PEGGY PORSCHEN
CAKES IN BLOOM

To my little family, Bryn and Max, for making me happy every day and always supporting me.
And to my parents for instilling my love for flowers.

PEGGY PORSCHEN

CAKES IN BLOOM

THE ART OF EXQUISITE
SUGARCRAFT FLOWERS

PHOTOGRAPHY BY GEORGIA GLYNN SMITH

Quadrille
PUBLISHING

CONTENTS

INTRODUCTION

When I discovered my love for cake decorating, I also became fascinated with hand-crafted sugar flowers: no other decoration complements a cake quite as beautifully. Not only do sugar flowers look stunning, they provide the perfect way to coordinate a cake with a special occasion. I am often asked to recreate a bride's bouquet in sugar to adorn her wedding cake, or to match the cake flowers to table centrepieces. Flowers speak a unique language and – just as cakes do – they make people happy.

Early in my career, I couldn't imagine being able to make realistic looking sugar flowers until in 2002 I enrolled in a basic sugar flower course. There I learned how to make wired roses with leaves, carnations and holly leaves with berries. It provided me with enough basic knowledge of the materials and techniques to develop my own skills and repertoire of blooms. I felt the best way to learn was to look at the real flower, so often I would take each one apart, petal by petal, and photograph the individual components. There are lots of different flower cutters on the market, but whenever I was unable to find the shape I needed, I would draw my own from the fresh petal and get cutters made or I would improvise by trimming a rose petal, for example, into the shape I wanted with a pair of fine craft scissors.

Since those early beginnings, it is impossible to count the number of flowers and petals I have made. But one thing I have learnt for certain is that only practice makes perfect (and even now, I would never say that my flowers are perfect). You will never stop learning, no matter how experienced you are. The most important thing is that you love flowers and that you enjoy yourself while making them. You may even find that crafting sugar flowers can be a form of therapy as it requires concentration while at the same time as being relaxing and the end result gives you an enormous sense of achievement, not to mention the reactions of excitement and amazement you will get from the people around you.

Within this book you will find a collection of contemporary and stylised sugar flowers, wired and unwired, to suit all skill levels. If you are new to flower making I recommend starting with a simple bloom such as a moulded rose or smaller blossoms, which are used in my Roses & Lily of the Valley or Tumbling Hydrangeas designs. If you have some experience already and would like to polish your skills and increase your repertoire, why not try the Spring Blossom Boutonnières, the Frangipanis or the Daisy Wreath. But if you are ready to set yourself a new challenge, I suggest you have a go at the Dahlia Café au Lait, the English Garden Roses or the pièce de la résistance of the book, the Floral Cascade. I am sure there will be plenty of choices and new designs for you to explore and I genuinely hope that this book will provide you with plenty of inspiration and guidance for many years to come.

If you are making sugar flowers as a regular hobby, you will get so much joy from seeing your own progress and the positive feedback from family and friends. Flowers, whether they are fresh or made from sugar, have a unique power to spread joy and happiness. If you have been making and decorating cakes for a while, but have never had the confidence to try making flowers, I hope that with the help and inspiration of this book, sugar flowers will quickly become your number one choice when cake decorating.

SUGAR FLOWER
BASICS

GETTING STARTED

Learning how to model sugar flowers is not only an enjoyable pastime but also a rewarding skill to master. If you are a complete novice, you may find it challenging at first, but with good preparation, plus patience and practice, you will be amazed at what you can achieve.

On the pages that follow is a brief introduction to the most important things you need to know before getting started. The variety of tools available can be overwhelming at first, but you don't need everything on my tool list to begin with. The lists opposite will provide you with an easy overview of the basic tools you need as a starter kit for almost any flower-making project, and a more specific list of specialist tools that you can purchase as and when required. There is also an essential guide to making and using flower paste, with a tried-and-tested recipe and helpful tips for trouble shooting.

Throughout this book you will find specialist terms and techniques that I will be referring to repeatedly. If you are accustomed to making sugar flowers in the UK it is likely that you are familiar with them. If not, please refer to my Sugar Flower Glossary on pages 219–221, where each term is explained in finer detail with accompanying images. If you are more or less a complete novice to the art of sugar flowers I recommend reading through this glossary first before starting to make any of the flowers in this book. It will help you to give you a good basic understanding of making sugar flowers and the specialist tools and techniques used.

BASIC TOOL KIT

Have the following items ready before making any type of sugar flowers (except flowers made with a silicone mould or roses moulded by hand).

Small non-stick plastic board with one smooth side and one veining/Mexican hat side (from Celcrafts)

Celpin – a rolling pin with a rounded end for balling and a cone-shaped end for frilling or modelling (from Celcrafts)

Sealable plastic bags – to store flower and sugar paste to prevent it from drying out

Stay-fresh mat – thick acetate sheet that stops flower paste from drying once it's been rolled out or a plastic sheet from an office supplies shop

Petal foam pad

Artist's paint palettes – it's good to have a few of these when making several flowers at a time. I use them for drying petals and blossoms or to mix colours

Cocktail sticks – to curve petal edges, hold flower buds and remove food paste colour from a tub

CUTTER CARE

Flower cutters are precious and can be expensive so you want them to last as long as possible. Cutters made of metal can rust when exposed to moisture, which is why most manufacturers recommend that you do not wash them in water. Personally, I prefer to clean my cutters properly as I find nothing more annoying that bits of dry flower paste contaminating my petals and leaves. This is how to protect your metal cutters from rust and still keep them clean:

Soak your used cutters in hot soapy water for about 30 minutes, then wash them thoroughly by hand. Place them on a baking tray lined with kitchen towel and let them dry in a hot – but switched off – oven (at about 100°C). Once dry, remove them from the oven and check that they are completely dry.

SPECIALIST TOOLS

The following items are more recipe specific:

'Sugarfacts' size guide for flower and modelling paste (from Celcrafts)
Non-stick veining board (from Culpitt)
Petal foam pad with holes – for Mexican hats
Perforated foam mat
Small plastic chocolate egg tray or apple tray (from any supermarket)
Silicone half-sphere moulds, 4cm and 6cm diameter (I use one from Formaflex)
Flower-drying trays (from Martellato)
Polystyrene cake dummies in various sizes – for drying wired flowers
Paper cupcake cases in various sizes – for drying large blooms
Flower stand for drying sugar flowers (from Orchard)
Polystyrene flower buds – pointed and round (I use Celbuds from Celcrafts)
Flower picks
Bone tool
Ball tool (from PME)
Dresden tool
Star tool
Veining tool (from Jem)
Veining modelling tool (from Jem)
Bulbous cone modelling tool
Celstick for frilling petal edges (from Celcrafts)
Tweezers
Selection of narrow and wide artist brushes – for dusting sugar flowers, leaves and petals
Selection of flower and leaf cutters
Selection of petal and leaf veiners
Selection of stamen
Selection of florist wires (greens and white)
White, nile green and brown florist tape
Small craft scissors
Strong wire scissors
Small palette knife
Small kitchen knives, plain edge and serrated

flower drying tray

ball tool

non-stick veining board

sugarcraft modelling tools

silicone flower mould (chrysanthemum)

plastic flower picks

food colour pen

artist's paintbrushes

metal flower cutters (cherry blossom)

petal dust

petal dust

perforated foam mat

stamen

florist tape

food paste colours

small craft scissors

silicone mould for flower centres

leaf veining mat

polystyrene ball

polystyrene buds

silicone half-sphere trays

flower veiner (hydrangea)

plunge cutter (daisy)

florist wires

plastic leaf cutters (rose leaf)

tweezers

leaf veining mats

non-stick plastic board with a smooth side and a veining/Mexican hat side

petal foam pad and acetate sheet/stay-fresh mat

non-stick veining board

1 2 3 4
5 6 7
8 9 10
11 12
13 14
15 16

size guide for flower & modelling paste

metal flower cutters (peony, peony leaf)

cel stick

celpin

FLOWER PASTE

Flower paste is a fine modelling paste made of icing sugar, egg white and a hardening agent such as gum tragacanth or gelatine. There are many different recipes available online and several sugarcraft suppliers sell ready-made flower paste or gum paste. My recommendation is to try some out to see which works best for you. From experience, the ideal type of flower paste depends on the weather conditions and the products available in the country in which you live. Hot and humid surroundings often require a paste that takes a little longer to dry, as it is used in air-conditioned kitchens where it can dry out very quickly. If your paste feels a little hard and dry to begin with, add a small amount of vegetable fat to make it smooth and more pliable.

What makes flower paste so special is that you can roll it out very thinly and create fine, detailed petals and leaves that look almost like fresh ones. Working with flower paste requires more care than sugar paste as it dries faster, and achieving the right consistency and using the right utensils is crucial in order to get satisfactory results.

Flower paste should always be kept inside a plastic bag, as it will dry out quickly when exposed to air. It can easily get contaminated with fibres from the air so avoid wearing dark fluffy clothing and thoroughly clean your work area and utensils before getting started. Needless to say, wash your hands and make sure you dry them completely before touching the flower paste, otherwise it can become wet and sticky.

INGREDIENTS

Makes 1kg

20g powdered gelatine
50ml cold water
1kg icing (confectioners') sugar
30g tylose powder (CMC)
25ml liquid glucose
30g white vegetable fat (shortening)
15g Meri-white mixed with 100ml water

METHOD

In a heatproof bowl, mix the gelatine with the 50ml cold water according to the manufacturer's instructions. Stand the bowl over a pan of hot (but not boiling) water and stir until the gelatine has dissolved. Add the glucose and vegetable fat then continue to stir over the heat until all the ingredients are melted and combined.

Sieve the icing sugar and gum tragacanth into the lightly greased mixing bowl of a heavy-duty electric mixer (the grease eases the strain on the machine). Add the gelatine mixture and Meri-white then mix slowly using a paddle attachment – at this stage it will be a beige colour. Once the mixture has come together, increase to a high speed and continue mixing until the paste becomes white and stretchy.

Rub a thin layer of vegetable fat over your hands and remove the paste from the bowl. Pull and stretch the paste several times, then knead it together on a surface lightly greased with vegetable fat until it forms a smooth paste. Wrap in a sealable plastic bag and leave to rest overnight at room temperature. This flower paste can be kept for up to one month.

tips Before rolling out flower paste, always knead thoroughly to make it smooth and pliable. Add a small amount of vegetable fat if the paste feels sticky.

It is possible to overwork flower paste, especially if you have very warm hands or if too much fat is added. If your paste has been overworked it will toughen up and become brittle very quickly. If this has happened, it is best to start again using a fresh piece of flower paste.

If the paste sticks to either the rolling pin or the plastic board, rub either with a thin layer of vegetable fat. If your paste becomes very wet and sticky, use a light dusting of cornflour instead of fat.

SUGAR FLOWER
DESIGNS

SPRING BLOSSOM BOUTONNIÈRES

INSPIRED BY A TRADITIONAL FLORAL
BUTTONHOLE, THIS SINGLE-TIER
ICED CAKE IS DRESSED WITH FLOWERS
THAT ARE PERFECTLY SUITED
TO A SPRINGTIME CELEBRATION.

INGREDIENTS

To make 1 daffodil, 2 ranunculus, 2 grape hyacinths,
2 primroses and a couple of leaves:

About 300g white flower paste

Small amount of white vegetable fat

Food paste colour in orange, lemon yellow, golden yellow, violet
(all from Wilton) and claret and spruce green (from Sugarflair)

Petal dust in yellow and spring green (from Rainbow)

Edible glue

2 white small pointed stamen

13 green 28-gauge florist wires, each cut into 4 even lengths
(for grape hyacinths)

1 white 26-gauge florist wire, cut in half (for primroses)

1 green 26-gauge florist wire, cut in half (for leaves)

1 white 24-gauge florist wire (only half is needed for 1 daffodil)

1 white 22-gauge florist wire, cut in half (for ranunculus)

White florist tape

Nile green florist tape

Small amount of soft-peak royal icing (see pages 216–17)
mixed with yellow food colour

About 50cm mint green satin ribbon, 5mm wide

EQUIPMENT

Basic tool kit (see page 11)

Daffodil flower-cutter set (from Culpitt or Peggy Porschen)

Small rose petal cutter (from Peggy Porschen)

Set of 3 round plunger cutters (from PME)

Small and medium primrose cutters (from FMM)

Small fantasy leaf cutter (from Sunflower SugarArt UK)

Paper piping bag

Dresden tool

Leaf veiner (multi-purpose)

Star tool

Bone tool

Ball tool

Frilling cone tool

Tweezers

Small polystyrene cake dummy

Wire scissors

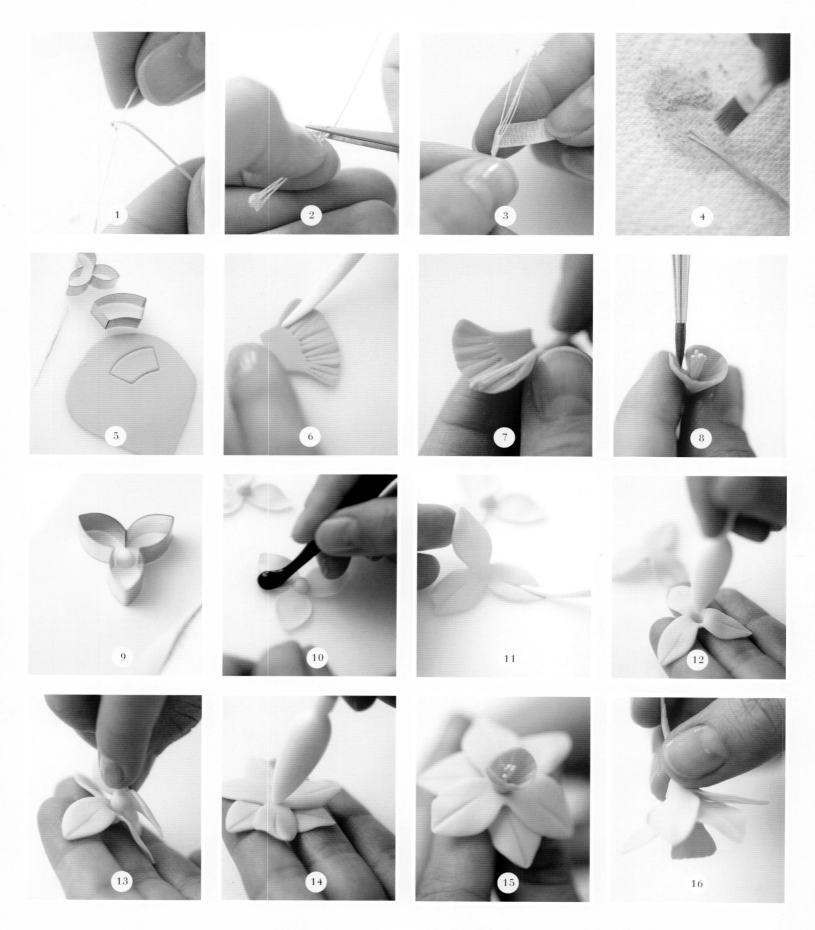

METHOD

you will need a cake 7.5cm in diameter and 5cm high, covered with marzipan and white sugar paste and trimmed with 15mm-wide mint green satin ribbon around the base.

MAKING THE DAFFODIL

Mix a hazelnut-sized piece of white flower paste with orange food paste colour.

Mix a walnut-sized piece of white flower paste with a mix of lemon yellow and golden yellow food paste colour.

Let the coloured flower pastes rest inside a plastic bag for about 15 minutes to firm up.

Take a length of 24-gauge wire, and, using tweezers, shape one end to form a small open hook (step 1).

Take 2 stamen, gather them in the middle and tuck the ends underneath the hook, then bend up (step 2). Close the hook firmly to hold the stamen in place.

Wrap the upper part of the wire and the hook holding the stamen with white florist tape (step 3).

Brush the stamen generously with yellow petal dust (step 4).

Roll out the orange paste until it is about 1mm thick. Cut out the shape for the daffodil throat using the curved rectangular cutter (step 5).

Place it on a foam pad. Using the wide end of the Dresden tool, emboss the longer side of the throat shape by running the tool from the middle to the edge (step 6). This will fan out the paste and give the frilly effect of a daffodil centre.

Brush the smooth part of the throat with edible glue and wrap it around the wire underneath the stamen (step 7).

Brush the edges of the paste with glue and stick them together (step 8). Leave to dry overnight.

Once dry, roll out the yellow flower paste over the largest possible Mexican hat for the daffodil petal cutter.

Turn the paste over and place the cutter centred over the Mexican hat to cut out the petal layer (step 9).

Repeat to make another layer of petals.

Place the layers on top of a foam pad, then widen the petals and thin the edges with a bone tool (step 10).

Turn each layer over and score down the middle of each petal with the thin end of a Dresden tool (step 11).

Push the tip of a frilling cone tool down the middle of each layer to make a well (step 12).

Brush the well in one layer with glue and centre the other layer on top so that the petals sit in between the petals in the first layer (step 13).

Push the middle down again with the frilling cone tool (see step 14).

Brush the well with edible glue and push the wire with the orange throat into the middle of the daffodil (step 15). Tuck the petals tightly underneath the throat (step 16).

Sit the flower inside the well of a perforated foam mat and place on top of a bowl or container to make room for the wire underneath the mat. Leave to dry overnight.

Once dry, tape the stem of the daffodil with nile green florist tape.

MAKING THE RANUNCULUS

Mix a piece of white flower paste about the size of 2 hazelnuts with lemon yellow food paste colour, then form it into 2 ball shapes.

Emboss 3 rings on top of each ball using the round plunger cutters.

Bend the ends of the 22-gauge wires to form an open hook, dip them in edible glue and push them into the bases of the balls (step 17). Leave to dry overnight.

Once dry, brush the tops of the balls lightly with green petal dust.

Mix about 75g of white flower paste with claret food paste colour to a bright pink.

Roll out the paste thinly and cut out 6 petals per ranunculus using the small rose petal cutter.

Place the petals on a foam pad and push a Celpin into the middle of each one to cup them (step 18).

Brush the bottom half of each petal with edible glue and stick them, one by one, around the yellow balls (step 19). The petals should overlap and the tips point towards the wire. The circle pattern on the yellow centres should still show.

To add the last petal, lift up the first petal from the top layer and tuck it underneath.

Make another 8 petals per flower and arrange them around the first layer of petals as before, but this time stick them around the centre in a more upright position so that the flowers begin to open up.

Mix the remaining pink paste with an equal amount of white flower paste to a pale pink.

Make another 10 petals for the next layer of each flower, and repeat the process as for the previous layer (step 20) followed by another 12 petals. Leave to dry overnight.

Once dry, tape the wires with green florist tape.

MAKING THE GRAPE HYACINTHS

Mix about 50g of white flower paste with violet food paste colour to a lilac shade.

Roll the lilac paste into a thin sausage and cut it into small pieces to make tiny balls 2mm and 3mm in diameter. For each flower you will need about 10 x 2mm balls and 20 x 3mm balls, so double the amount to make 2 grape hyacinths.

Keep the balls tightly wrapped in a plastic bag until use, to prevent the paste from drying.

Shape each ball into a teardrop (step 21).

Dip the end of a green 28-gauge wire in edible glue, insert it into the tip of the first teardrop and push it in about halfway (step 22).

Repeat for the remaining teardrops. Leave to dry overnight.

Once dry, bunch together 1 bud with 3 more underneath and secure with green florist tape (step 23).

Build up the layers by adding more buds in between and underneath the previous layer, increasing the size as you move down. Bend the buds out slightly and arrange them half over the previous layer to form a grape shape (step 24).

Once all the buds have been added, tape all the way down the wire and trim the end of the stem with wire scissors.

Repeat to make the second flower.

MAKING THE PRIMROSES

Roll out a small amount of white flower paste over a large and medium Mexican hat hole.

Cut out 1 medium and 1 small primrose blossom using the primrose cutters.

Place each blossom onto a foam pad with the Mexican hat facing down. Thin out the petals and widen the edges with a bone tool.

Push a 5-sided star tool into the centre of each blossom (step 25).

Bend one end of the white 26-gauge wires into a small hook using tweezers.

Brush the centres with edible glue and push a wire into the middle of each until the hooks are submerged in the Mexican hats (step 26).

Pinch the paste of the Mexican hats down the wires to create a long neck.

Hang the blossoms over a polystyrene dummy. Leave to dry overnight.

Once dry, brush the centres lightly with spring green petal dust (step 27).

Put the yellow royal icing into a paper piping bag and pipe a small dot in the middle of each primrose to cover the hooks (step 28).

Wrap green florist tape around the wire of each primrose.

MAKING THE LEAVES

Mix a small amount of white flower paste with spruce green food paste colour to a pale green.

Roll out the pale green paste over a veining board until it is about 1mm thick.

Flip the paste over and cut out 2 leaf shapes with the thick end of the pencil vein starting at the bottom of the cutter and the thinner part of the vein going through the top (step 29).

Ball the edges with a ball tool (step 30).

Dip the ends of the green 26-gauge wires in edible glue and insert one into the bottom of each pencil vein. Push the wires one-third of the way into the leaf.

Emboss each leaf using a leaf veiner (step 31).

Pinch the leaf tips with your fingers (step 32) and place them on a perforated foam mat. Leave to dry overnight.

Once dry, tape up the wires with nile green florist tape.

TO ASSEMBLE THE FLOWERS AND LEAVES

Bunch the wires together to make a bouquet and tie with the mint green ribbon. Carefully place it on top of the iced cake.

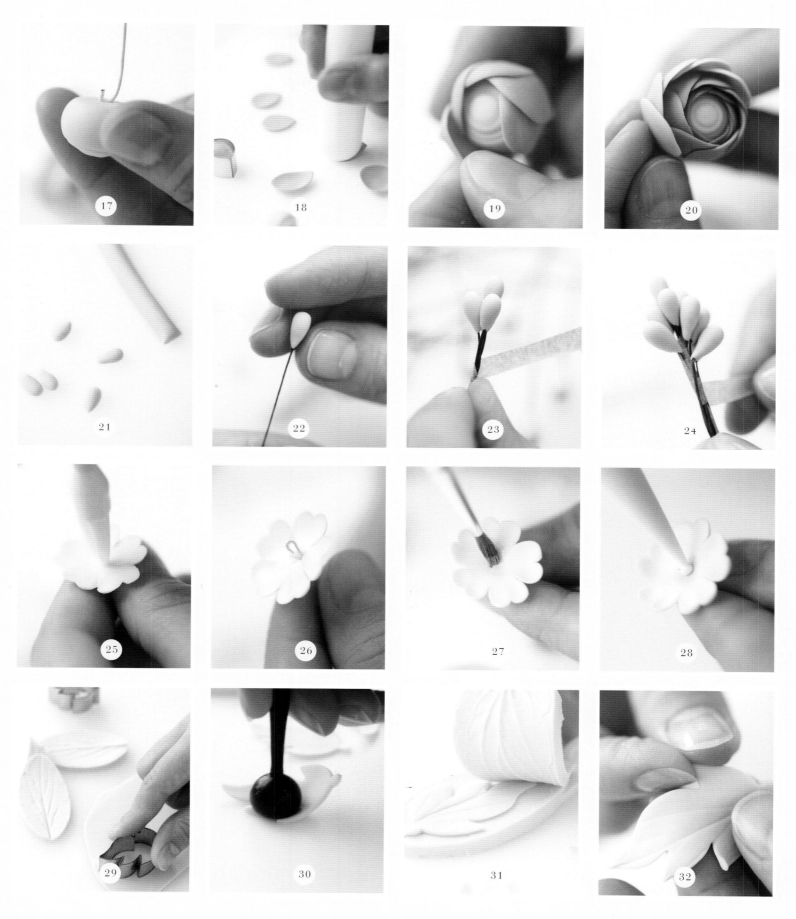

PURPLE PANSIES

WITH AN IRRESISTIBLE FLAVOUR
COMBINATION OF CHOCOLATE AND
VIOLET, THESE EDIBLE BEAUTIES
ARE INSPIRED BY THE FLORAL WINDOW
BOXES OF BELGRAVIA IN LONDON.
EACH INDIVIDUAL MINIATURE CAKE IS
DECORATED WITH A SINGLE EXQUISITE
PALE VIOLET PANSY.

INGREDIENTS

To make 12 cakes with purple pansies:

30cm-square chocolate cake

400g buttercream

Violet extract to taste (I used about 1 teaspoon)

About 250g white flower paste

Food paste colour in violet (from Wilton)

Craft dust in ultramarine (from Sugarflair)

Petal dust in black magic and primrose (from Rainbow)

Small amount of white vegetable fat

Small amount of vodka

Cornflour in a muslin pouch, for dusting

EQUIPMENT

Basic tool kit (see page 11)

Large pansy petal cutter set (from Peggy Porschen)

Plastic piping bag

1.5cm-diameter piping tube

Veining stick

Celstick

Flower drying tray

Very fine artist's brush

METHOD

Mix the white flower paste with some of the violet food paste colour to a lilac shade. If the paste feels stiff and sticky, add a dab of vegetable fat and knead together until the paste becomes smooth and pliable. Keep inside a sealable plastic bag to prevent it drying out.

Roll out some of the lilac paste until it is about 1mm thick and cut out some petal shapes (step 1). For each pansy you will need 2 small and 2 large teardrop-shaped petals and 1 large petal shape. You will need 1 pansy per cake; 12 in total.

Place the petal shapes for the first pansy on a foam pad (keep the remaining rolled-out paste covered with an acetate sheet to prevent the paste from drying out).

To make the petals curl up slightly, ball them (see page 219) using a Celpin (step 2).

Roll the veining stick across each petal with the thin end of the stick pointing towards the thinnest part of the petal each time (step 3). Use a reasonable amount of pressure to emboss the petal veins.

Lightly dust a plastic board with cornflour. Lay the petals on the board and frill the edges with a Celstick (step 4).

To assemble the flower, brush the right side of one large teardrop with a small amount of edible glue (step 5) and stick the other large teardrop petal next to it, slightly overlapping.

Brush the bottom edge of both petals with a small amount of edible glue and attach the 2 smaller teardrop petals, slightly overlapping the large petals (step 6).

Pinch the narrow end of the largest petal to a tip (step 7), brush the middle of the pansy with edible glue and attach the petal, using the blunt end of a very fine artist's brush, so that it is centred underneath the 4 teardrop petals (step 8).

Place the pansy flower into the well of a flower drying tray (step 9) and repeat for the remaining pansies. Leave to dry overnight.

Once the petals have dried, dust the outer edges of the pansies with ultramarine craft dust (step 10).

Dust the pansy centres with primrose petal dust (step 11).

Mix the black petal dust with a drop of vodka to form a thick paint and, using a very fine artist's paintbrush, paint lines from the centre outwards along each petal (step 12).

Mix the buttercream with violet food paste colour to a medium lilac shade and flavour with violet extract to taste.

Attach the round piping tube to the front of a plastic piping bag and transfer the buttercream to the bag.

Sandwich together 2 chocolate cake layers with a blob of buttercream. Pipe another blob of buttercream on top of the cake and place a pansy in the centre.

Repeat for the remaining cakes.

FRANGIPANIS

NOTHING EVOKES THAT TROPICAL FEELING QUITE LIKE THE WARM YELLOW-CENTRED FRANGIPANI, UNIVERSALLY LOVED BECAUSE OF ITS SWEET SCENT AND SHEER BEAUTY. THE SUGAR BLOOMS LOOK SENSATIONAL ON THIS PAINTED AQUA AND WHITE STRIPED SINGLE-TIER CAKE.

INGREDIENTS

To make about 3 large, 2 medium and 2 small frangipanis:

About 300g white flower paste

Small amount of white vegetable fat

Food paste colour in teal (from Wilton)

Petal dust in primrose and tangerine (both from Sugarflair)

Edible glue

Small amount of soft-peak royal icing (see pages 216–17)

EQUIPMENT

Basic tool kit (see page 11)

Frangipani petal cutter set (from Tinkertech Two)

Ball tool

Selection of regular and small cupcake paper cases

Paper piping bag

to recreate the cake you will need a cake 10cm in diameter and 10cm high, covered with marzipan and white sugar paste. While the icing is soft, emboss the sides of the cake with horizontal lines about 2.5cm apart using the back of a kitchen knife. Let the icing set and paint the cake with stripes of aqua food colour. When the colour is dry, place the cake on a 15cm-diameter drum covered with white sugar paste and put 15mm-wide aqua blue satin ribbon around the edge.

Roll out the white flower paste to a thickness of about 2mm. Cut out 5 petals for each flower using the same size frangipani cutter for each petal (step 1).

Place the petals on the foam pad and push the ball tool along the centre of the petals (step 2). The edges should remain thick while the inner part of the petals should curve to form a cup shape.

Brush the right side of one petal with edible glue and place another petal over the top so that it overlaps by one-third (step 3).

Continue for the remaining petals and fan them out (step 4). All the petals should meet at the bottom.

Place the pointed end of the Celpin where the petals meet, then roll the petal fan into a cone shape (step 5).

Pinch the bottom of the petals together so they open into a flower (step 6).

Trim the excess paste off the bottom (step 7) and place in a paper cup (step 8).

Repeat for the remaining frangipani flowers. Leave to dry overnight.

Once dry, dust the flower centres with primrose petal dust, from the centre to about halfway along each petal. Mix a little tangerine with primrose petal dust and dust the flower centres to give them a warm orangey hue (step 9).

Steam the flowers for about 3 seconds to set the colour and give them a satin-like sheen.

Put the royal icing in a piping bag and use it to stick the frangipanis to the top of the cake.

CARNATION POMANDERS

THESE UNIQUE CONFECTIONS ARE
INSPIRED BY THE ELEGANT FLOWER
POMANDERS OFTEN CARRIED BY
BRIDESMAIDS AT SUMMER WEDDINGS.
DENSELY DECORATED WITH
CARNATIONS, THEY MAKE A
STUNNING CENTREPIECE.

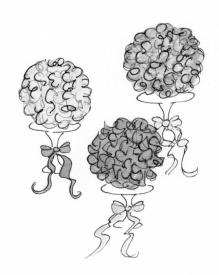

INGREDIENTS

To make about 40 carnations per cake:

About 2.4kg white flower paste

Small amount of white vegetable fat

Food paste colour in lemon yellow, golden yellow, peach, orange (all from Wilton)

and red extra (from Sugarflair)

Petal dust in apricot, pink and permanent rose (all from Sugarflair)

Edible glue

150g soft-peak royal icing (see pages 216–17)

Cornflour in a muslin pouch, for dusting

EQUIPMENT

Basic tool kit (see page 11)

Small and medium carnation cutters (25mm and 35mm from PME or FMM)

Small Celpin

Frilling cone tool

Flower stand (or use a perforated foam mat)

3 paper piping bags

METHOD

---

to recreate the cake you will need
3 cakes baked in 15cm spherical cake tins.
Each cake is covered with marzipan and sugar
paste in either yellow, peach or coral red.

Divide the white flower paste into 3 equal
parts and mix 1 batch with lemon yellow and
golden yellow food colour, 1 with orange and
red extra to achieve a coral red shade and one
with peach. If the paste feels sticky, add a dab
of vegetable fat.

Place the pastes inside plastic bags and allow
to rest for at least 15 minutes.

MAKING THE CARNATIONS
Each carnation is made up of 2 small petal
layers and 1 medium petal layer. You will
need 40 yellow, 40 peach and 40 coral red
carnations. Roll out some of the flower paste
until 1mm thick.

Cut out a carnation petal layer using the small
carnation cutter (step 1). Clean the petal edges
with your finger to ensure a sharp cut (step 2)
and place the petal layer on a plastic board
lightly dusted with cornflour.

Frill the petal edges using a small Celpin
(step 3).

Push the round end of the frilling cone tool
into the petal centre (step 4) and pinch the
frills together to form a rosette (step 5).

Place the rosette in a well of the flower stand
(step 6) and leave to dry for a few hours.

Repeat for the remaining carnations.

Once dry, repeat this process for the next petal
layer using the same size carnation cutter and
flower paste colour.

Once frilled, brush the middle of the carnation
petals with edible glue and stick the first
petals on top (steps 7 and 8).

Place the carnation back on the flower stand
and leave to dry. Repeat for all the remaining
carnations.

To add the final layer, repeat the same process
again using the medium carnation cutter.
Leave to dry overnight.

DUSTING THE FLOWERS
Brush the edges of the yellow and peach
carnations with a blend of apricot and pink
petal dust (step 9), and the coral red carnation
with permanent rose petal dust.

STEAMING THE FLOWERS
Steam each carnation for about 3 seconds to
set the colours and give them a satin-like sheen.

TO DECORATE THE CAKES
Place each ball-shaped cake onto a cake stand
or plate. Divide the royal icing into 3 portions
and mix each part with the appropriate colour
to match the icing of the cake.

Pipe a dab of royal icing at the back of each
carnation and stick them around the cake of
the same colour, starting at the bottom and
working your way up. Keep them as close
together as possible to avoid large gaps.
If you do find there are gaps that you would
like to hide, make a few small rosettes to stick
in between the carnations.

ROSES & LILY OF THE VALLEY

THIS IS A CLASSICAL FLORAL
COMBINATION, PLUCKED FROM AN
ENGLISH COUNTRY GARDEN.
LILY OF THE VALLEY, SMALL AND
SPRINKLED LIKE DELICATE DROPLETS,
IS PAIRED WITH MOULDED ROSES
IN SOFT PINK HUES.

INGREDIENTS

To make 1 large single-tier cake and 3 miniature cakes:

About 500g white flower paste

About 300g white sugar paste

Food paste colour in claret and moss green (from Sugarflair)

Small amount of white vegetable fat

About 150g royal icing (see pages 216–17)

EQUIPMENT

Basic tool kit (see page 11)

Large and small lily of the valley blossom cutters (from FMM)

Medium and small rose leaf cutters (from PME)

Multipurpose leaf cutter, 15 x 35mm (from Peggy Porschen)

Rose leaf veiner (from Diamond Paste)

Dresden tool

Tiny ball tool (from PME)

Scissors

Plastic sleeve (from any office stationery supplier)

2 paper piping bags

to recreate the cakes For the large cake shown on page 45, you will need a cake 20cm in diameter and 10cm high, covered with marzipan and white sugar paste, trimmed around the base with 15mm-wide pink satin ribbon. The 25cm cake board is covered with white sugar paste and also has 15mm-wide pink satin ribbon around the edge.

You will also need 3 miniature cakes, 5cm in diameter and 5cm high, covered with marzipan and a mixture of white, pale pink and pistachio green sugar paste.

You will need about 8 large, 6 medium and 6 small rosebuds, 6 rose petals, 6 medium and 6 small rose leaves, 100 large and 65 small Lily of the Valley blossoms and 20 leaves.

MAKING THE ROSES AND BUDS

To make the roses, mix 250g of white flower paste with 250g of white sugar paste until smooth and pliable. If the paste feels sticky, add a dab of vegetable fat.

Mix half the paste with claret food paste colour to a light pink shade, a quarter to a medium pink shade and the other quarter to a dark pink. Wrap the pastes in plastic bags for about 30 minutes until firm.

Cut the hole-punched edge off the plastic sleeve with a pair of scissors and rub the inside thinly with white vegetable fat.

MAKING THE ROSEBUDS

To make 1 medium rosebud you will need 3 hazelnut-sized ball shapes in medium pink

and 1 dark pink oval shape for the rose centre. Place them inside the plastic sleeve (using half of the sleeve), leaving about 2.5cm between the balls. To save time, try to fit enough paste for about 3 buds inside the sleeve.

Fold the other half of the plastic sleeve over the top and lightly flatten each piece of paste with the palm of your hand to prevent them from rolling around (step 1).

To shape the paste into petals, rub your thumb over each piece in a circular motion until the paste is 2–3mm thick (step 2).

Continue to flatten the side facing the crease of the plastic sleeve to form a half-moon shape; the edge of the paste should be thin and sharp, while the remaining part of the petal stays thick. Keeping this part of the paste thick is important as it gives the petal strength. If the paste gets too thin, the petal will collapse and not hold up its shape.

Repeat for all the ball shapes.

Flatten the oval paste in the same way, maintaining its oval shape. Open the plastic sleeve and take out an oval petal. Curl it into a spiral with the thin edge at the top (step 3).

Pick up one of the round petals, curve it to form a cup and lay it over the open side of the spiral (step 4). It should sit about 1mm higher than the top edge of the centre.

Fold the paste down on the left, then tuck another petal under the right-hand side, followed by another (step 5).

Curl back the edges of the outer petals and pinch the tops into a soft tip. Pinch off the excess paste at the base and let the rosebud set.

Repeat for the remaining 5 medium and 6 small rosebuds (using smaller pieces of paste).

MAKING LARGE ROSES

To make the 8 large roses, repeat as for the rosebuds, then make another 4 light pink petals for the outer layer. These should be slightly larger than the 3 petals of the previous layer (step 6).

Arrange the 4 petals around the rosebud in the same manner as for the previous layers – they should sit about 3mm higher than the layer of 3 petals and evenly interlock (step 7).

Tightly tuck the right-hand side of each petal against the rosebud and pinch the bottom to give the rose a rounded base.

Curl back the outer petal edges and pinch the tips softly (step 8). Pinch off the excess paste at the base and put the rose aside to set (step 9).

Repeat this process for the remaining 7 roses.

MAKING THE ROSE PETALS

Use the leftover pale pink paste to make a few rose petals. Take 6 pieces of paste (smaller than a hazelnut), put them in the plastic sleeve and shape as for the rosebuds, using your thumb.

Pinch up each petal at the thicker end (the bottom) and curl down the thinner top edge with a soft pinch. Leave the petals to set for about 1 hour.

MAKING LILY OF THE VALLEY BLOSSOMS

Knead the white flower paste with a small amount of vegetable fat until it is smooth and pliable.

Roll out a strip of paste until it is about 1mm thick, with Mexican hats to suit the sizes of the lily of the valley cutters; they should be as large as possible to create the bell shapes.

Cut out a few blossoms at a time (step 10) and place them on a foam mat.

Press a tiny ball tool into the centre of each petal so that the paste curves up (step 11).

Turn the blossom over and hollow out the Mexican hat (step 12).

Repeat for a total of 100 large and 65 small blossoms and leave to set (step 13).

MAKING THE LEAVES

Mix the remaining white flower paste with moss green food paste colour to make a light green. Roll out the paste until it is about 1mm thick (step 14).

Cut out 6 medium and 6 small rose leaves and press them in the rose leaf veiner.

Place the leaves curved over a perforated foam mat and allow to set.

Roll out the remaining green paste and cut out 20 lily of the valley leaves using the multipurpose leaf cutter (step 15); 10 leaves should point to the left and 10 to the right.

Place the leaves on a foam pad and run the thin end of a Dresden tool down the centres to emboss a line (step 16).

Place the leaves curved over a perforated foam mat and leave to set (step 17).

TO DECORATE THE CAKES

Mix half of the royal icing with green food colour to the same shade as the leaves. Add a little water if required to make a soft-peak consistency, then transfer to a piping bag.

Put the remaining white royal icing into a piping bag; this should have a stiffer consistency. Divide the top of the large cake into 6 even sections, tilt the cake slightly away from you, then pipe a few green curved stems from the cake edge, down the side and towards the middle of the cake in each section (step 18).

You can vary the sizes and shapes of the stems for a more relaxed, natural look.

Cover the join of two piped stems with a large rose, accompanied by leaves and rosebuds, using the stiff white icing (steps 19 and 20).

Stick the lily of the valley leaves to either side of the tops of the stems, then arrange the blossoms, starting with the larger ones at the top then placing the smaller ones towards the bottom (step 21).

To decorate the miniature cakes, using the white royal icing attach a large rose to the top of the green and white cake and position a few petals so they are falling down the sides.

Pipe 2 green stems down the side of the pink miniature cake.

Stick 2 leaves on either side of the stems, over the edge of the cake, then arrange the blossoms down the stems to match the design of the large cake.

SNOWBALLS

ON A WALK THROUGH LONDON'S
BATTERSEA PARK, I PASSED A
BEAUTIFUL SHRUB WITH SMALL
POMPOM-LIKE FLOWERS. THIS WAS
MY INSPIRATION FOR THESE
INDIVIDUAL SPHERICAL BOUQUETS
OF SNOWY WHITE BLOOMS PERCHED
ATOP CHIC MINIATURE
ICED CAKES.

INGREDIENTS

To make 3 snowballs with leaves:
About 100g white sugar paste
About 150g white flower paste
Small amount of white vegetable fat
Food paste colour in spruce green (from Sugarflair)
Edible glue
About 50g royal icing (see pages 216–17)

EQUIPMENT

Basic tool kit (see page 11)
Small 5-petal blossom cutter (size 3/12mm, from Peggy Porschen)
Small multipurpose leaf cutter
(15 x 35mm, part of a 5-piece cutter set from Peggy Porschen)
Lily leaf veiner (from Diamond Paste)
Bone tool
5-sided star tool
Paper piping bag

METHOD

to recreate the cakes you will need 3 miniature cakes measuring 5cm in diameter and 5cm high, covered with marzipan and white sugar paste and trimmed with 15mm-wide satin ribbon.

Divide the white sugar paste into 3 equal-sized pieces (weighing just over 30g each) and shape each one into a ball.

Brush the top of each cake with edible glue and stick a sugar paste ball on top (step 1).

Knead the white flower paste until smooth and pliable. If the paste feels sticky, add a small dab of vegetable fat.

On a plastic board with a suitably sized hole for a Mexican hat, roll out a small amount of the flower paste to a thickness of about 1mm.

Centre the blossom cutter over the Mexican hat and stamp out a blossom shape.

Place the blossom – Mexican hat-side up – on a foam pad and press a small bone tool on each petal to flatten (step 2).

Push a 5-sided star tool into the middle of the blossom and push the petal edges against the sides of the tool to emboss with lines (step 3). Should the star tool stick to the paste, rub it lightly with vegetable fat.

Repeat for a total of 30 blossoms per cake – 90 in total – and leave to dry for a few hours.

Meanwhile, mix the remaining white flower paste with a small amount of spruce green food colour to make a pale green shade.

Roll out the paste to a thickness of about 1mm and cut out 2 leaves per cake using the multipurpose leaf cutter (step 4).

Press each leaf in the lily leaf veiner (step 5), then lay them curved over a perforated foam mat (step 6) and leave to dry for a few hours.

Put the royal icing in a piping bag and attach 2 leaves to the edge of each cake (step 7).

Stick a ring of blossoms around the base of each ball using royal icing (step 8) and work your way up each of the balls until they are completely covered with blossoms (step 9).

DAHLIA CAFÉ
AU LAIT

AT ONCE ROMANTIC AND MODERN,
A TRIO OF THESE GLORIOUSLY
INTRICATE BLOOMS ARE DRAMATICALLY
POSITIONED ON CRISP, ANGULAR
CAPPUCCINO-COLOURED TIERS.

INGREDIENTS

To make 2 large dahlias and 1 medium dahlia:
About 600g white flower paste
Small amount of white vegetable fat
Food paste colour in dusky pink (from Sugarflair) and ivory (from Wilton)
Petal dust in dusky pink (from Rainbow) and Champagne (from Sugarflair)
Edible glue
Royal icing (see pages 216–17)

EQUIPMENT

Basic tool kit (see page 11)
Medium daisy plunger cutter (from PME)
Rose petal cutter (from Peggy Porschen)
Flower-centre mould (from Diamond Paste)
Dahlia petal veiner (I used one from Petal Crafts)
Dresden tool
Polystyrene cake dummy

METHOD

to recreate the cake you will need a stacked 2-tier square cake with the following dimensions:

top tier: 15cm across x 12.5cm high

bottom tier: 20cm across x 12.5cm high

You will also need a 25cm-square cake drum. All tiers are covered with marzipan and caffè latte-coloured sugar paste (I used dark brown food colour from Sugarflair mixed with ivory sugar paste) and trimmed around the sides with 25mm-wide pink grosgrain ribbon and 10mm-wide pale pink satin ribbon. The cake drum is covered with caffè latte-coloured sugar paste and is trimmed around the edge with 15mm-wide bridal white satin ribbon.

Mix about 200g of the white flower paste with dusky pink food paste colour and a tiny amount of ivory to make a pale creamy dusky pink shade. Mix the remaining 400g with ivory food paste colour and a tiny amount of dusky pink to make a pale cream shade with a hue of pink. Place the pastes inside plastic bags and let them rest for at least 15 minutes.

MAKING THE FLOWER CENTRES

Using some of the dusky pink flower paste, make 3 ball shapes with a diameter of about 1cm and push one of the balls into the second-largest well of the flower-centre mould.

Dip the tip of a cocktail stick in edible glue and push it into the ball, then shape and smooth the paste against the cocktail stick (step 1). Remove the ball from the mould and repeat with the other 2 balls. Leave to dry overnight.

MAKING THE BUDS

Roll out the remaining dusky pink paste to a thickness of 1mm. Cut out 1 daisy shape per flower centre and place them on a foam pad (step 2).

Run the wider end of a Dresden tool along each petal from the outer edge to the base, so they curve up slightly (step 3).

Brush the daisy shape thinly with edible glue. Push the cocktail stick of the flower centre through the middle of the daisy shape (step 4). Fold alternate petals over the flower centre (step 5). Then fold the remaining petals over in the same way. Leave the cocktail stick in place.

Repeat steps 2–5 to add another 2 petal layers to each flower centre (step 6) and leave each layer to dry for at least 2 hours.

MAKING THE PETALS

Add 100g of ivory–pink flower paste to the leftover dusky pink paste and roll it out to a thickness of 1mm. Cut out several petals using the dahlia/rose petal cutter and place them on a foam pad.

Thin the petal edges with a Celpin and slightly stretch out the petal tips (step 7).

Press the dahlia petal veiner on top of each petal to emboss (step 8). Roll the bottom of each petal into a little curl, pinch the petal tip and curl it back slightly (step 9).

Repeat steps 7–9 to make 12–14 petals for the first layer of each dahlia.

Use your finger to flatten the base of each petal slightly, then brush them with edible glue.

Stick the petals evenly around the bud with the tips pointing outward and the open part of the petal at the same level as the top of the bud (step 10). Leave them to set for a couple of hours before adding another layer of petals.

Repeat to make another layer of petals, increasing the number of petals by about 2. Arrange them in the gaps between the petals in the previous row (step 11).

Repeat to make the final layer of petals of 2 of the dahlias, again increasing the number of petals by about 2. Leave them to dry completely, ideally overnight.

DUSTING THE FLOWERS

Dust the inner petals with a blend of Champagne and dusky pink petal dust, and the bud with a more pinky shade (step 12). The overall colour should gradually become paler as you work towards the outside of the flower.

STEAMING THE FLOWERS

Steam each dahlia for about 3 minutes to set the colour and give the paste a satin-like sheen.

TO DECORATE THE CAKE

Pipe a dab of royal icing onto the back of each flower, then push the cocktail stick at the back of each flower into the cake.

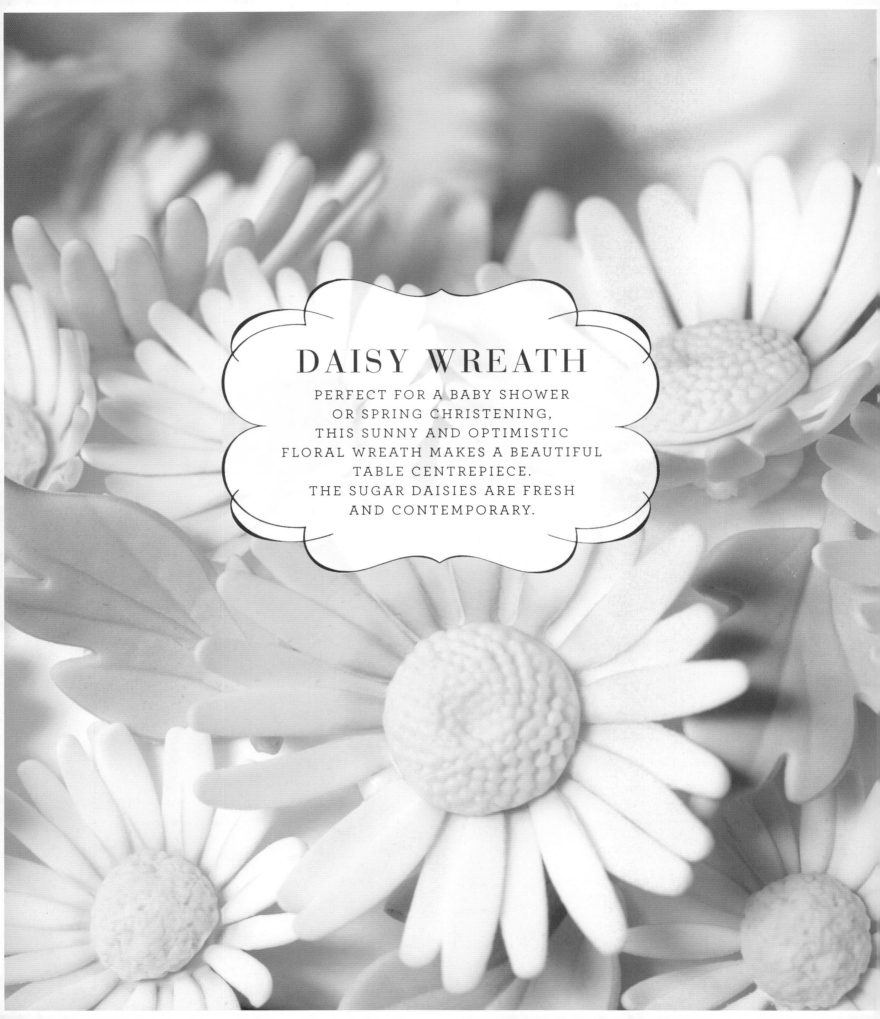

DAISY WREATH

PERFECT FOR A BABY SHOWER
OR SPRING CHRISTENING,
THIS SUNNY AND OPTIMISTIC
FLORAL WREATH MAKES A BEAUTIFUL
TABLE CENTREPIECE.
THE SUGAR DAISIES ARE FRESH
AND CONTEMPORARY.

INGREDIENTS

To make about 15 large, 15 medium and 20 small daisies
and about 10 small and 10 large leaves:

About 500g white flower paste

Small amount of white vegetable fat

Food paste colour in lemon yellow and moss green (from Wilton)

Petal dust in spring green (from Rainbow)

Cornflour inside a muslin pouch, for dusting

Edible glue

Small amount of royal icing (see pages 216–17)

EQUIPMENT

Basic tool kit (see page 11)

Daisy petal cutter set, 3 middle-sized cutters only (from FMM)

Small and medium fantasy leaf cutters (from Sunflower Sugar Art)

Flower-centre mould (from Diamond Paste)

Lily leaf veiner (from Diamond Paste)

Ball tool

Dresden tool

Silicone tray with 4cm half-sphere moulds

Paper piping bag

DAISY 68 WREATH

METHOD

to recreate the cake you will need a sponge cake baked in a 23cm-diameter garland ring mould (I used one from Alan Silverwood) covered with marzipan and white sugar paste. Before decorating, place the sponge on a cake stand (you may wish to place a 23cm-diameter cake card on the stand as a base for the cake).

MAKING THE DAISIES

Knead the white flower paste until it is smooth and pliable; if it feels firm and sticky, add a dab of vegetable fat. Roll out some of the paste on a plastic board until it is very thin (less than 1mm thick). Rub a thin layer of vegetable fat over the paste to help prevent the cutter from sticking to the paste at the next stage.

Cut out 2 daisy shapes of the same size using a daisy petal cutter. As the petals are very fine and thin, press the cutter firmly onto the paste and peel away the excess. Turn the cutter over and clean the petal edges with your finger.

Use the small tool that is part of the cutter set to push each petal out of the cutter (step 1).

Place the daisy shapes on a foam pad and flatten the centre with a ball tool (step 2).

Run the wider end of a Dresden tool from the edge of each petal to the base, to make them curl up slightly (step 3).

Place 1 daisy shape in the well of a half-sphere mould – or paint palette if it's a small daisy – dusted with cornflour.

Brush the centre of the daisy with edible glue and place the second daisy shape on top with the petals placed in the gaps between the petals of the first shape (step 4).

If necessary, use the Dresden tool to space out the petals evenly.

Repeat this process for the remaining daisies and leave to dry overnight.

Mix about 50g of white flower paste with yellow food paste colour to make a pale yellow shade and roll out about 30 balls measuring 7mm in diameter and about 20 balls measuring 5mm in diameter.

Push the 7mm balls into the fifth-largest flower-centre mould and the 5mm balls into the second smallest mould (step 5).

Once the daisy shapes are dry, brush the centres and the bottoms of the petals with green petal dust (step 6).

Brush the daisy centres with edible glue and stick the yellow balls on top (step 7); use the large balls for the large and medium daisies and the small balls for the small daisies.

MAKING THE LEAVES

Mix the remaining white flower paste with green food paste colour to make a pale green shade. Roll out the paste to a thickness of about 1mm, then cut out 15 medium and 15 small leaf shapes using the fantasy leaf cutters.

Place the leaves on a foam pad and thin the edges with a ball tool (step 8).

Press each leaf in the leaf veiner (step 9).

Pinch the leaf tips with your fingers (step 10) and lay them curved on a perforated foam mat to dry (step 11).

TO DECORATE THE CAKE

Put the royal icing in a paper piping bag and pipe a blob on the back of each daisy, then stick it onto the cake (step 12). Start by spacing out the larger daisies over the top, then fill the gaps on the inside of the ring with smaller daisies and continue to cover the outer edge.

Arrange the pale green leaves in the gaps between the daisies.

TUMBLING HYDRANGEAS

A SHOW-STOPPING FIVE-TIER WEDDING CAKE DECORATED WITH BEAUTIFUL HYDRANGEA BLOOMS. THE SECRET TO ACHIEVING SUCH REALISTIC RESULTS LIES IN THE PETAL DUST THAT IS BRUSHED ALONG THE PETAL EDGES ONCE THEY ARE DRY.

ROSES & VIOLETS

INSPIRED BY A VINTAGE
CHINA TEA CUP, THIS IS A LOVELY
DESIGN TO CHOOSE FOR A FIRST
SUGAR FLOWER PROJECT.

INGREDIENTS

To make 2 large roses, 3 rosebuds, about 18 violets and 9 white blossoms:

About 150g white flower paste

About 100g white sugar paste

White vegetable fat

Food paste colour in claret (from Sugarflair), violet, moss green and lemon yellow (from Wilton)

Food colour pen in black (from Rainbow)

About 1 tablespoon of royal icing

3 cupcakes (sponge flavoured to your choice (see page 200)

About 100g lemon buttercream (see page 203)

EQUIPMENT

Basic tool kit (see page 11)

Small violet blossom cutter (from Tinkertech Two)

Small 5-petal blossom cutter (from Peggy Porschen)

Ball tool (from PME)

Frilling cone tool

Scissors

Small palette knife

Plastic sleeve (from any office stationery supplier)

2 paper piping bags

MAKING THE WHITE BLOSSOMS

Knead the remaining white flower paste until it is smooth and pliable.

Using the 5-petal blossom cutter, make about 36 white blossoms following the same process as for the violets, up to and including the setting stage (steps 10–12).

Mix a tiny amount of royal icing with yellow food colour to form a soft-peak consistency (add a little water if necessary), then transfer to a paper piping bag.

MAKING THE VIOLETS

Mix the remaining white flower paste with violet food paste colour.

Roll out a strip of paste to a thickness of about 1mm, with small Mexican hats.

Cut out several violet blossoms with a Mexican hat in the middle of each one, then place them on a foam pad, Mexican hat side up.

Press a tiny ball tool onto each petal so that the paste curls up (step 13).

Turn a blossom over and push the tip of a frilling cone tool into the centre to create a well.

Repeat for the remaining blossoms and leave to dry until set.

Once set, draw thin black lines on the centre petal and the 2 adjacent petals using the food colour pen (step 14).

Use the remaining yellow royal icing to pipe a small dot in the centre of each blossom.

Snip a small hole in the tip of the bag and pipe a dot of icing in the blossom centres. Drag the icing along the large petal before you lift off the tip of the piping bag to create a pointy centre (step 15).

TO DECORATE THE CUPCAKES

Using a palette knife, spread the buttercream in a dome shape over the tops of the cupcakes. Chill for about 15 minutes to firm up the buttercream slightly.

Meanwhile, mix the remaining royal icing with moss green food paste colour and transfer to a paper piping bag.

Attach a rose or 3 rosebuds to the top of each cupcake by pushing them into the buttercream.

Snip off the tip of the piping bag in a 'V' shape (step 16), then pipe several leaves around the roses by wiggling the bag up and down as you squeeze out the icing. Just before you pull the piping bag away, stop squeezing to form a nice leaf tip (step 17).

While the green icing is still wet, arrange some violets and blossoms around the roses (step 18).

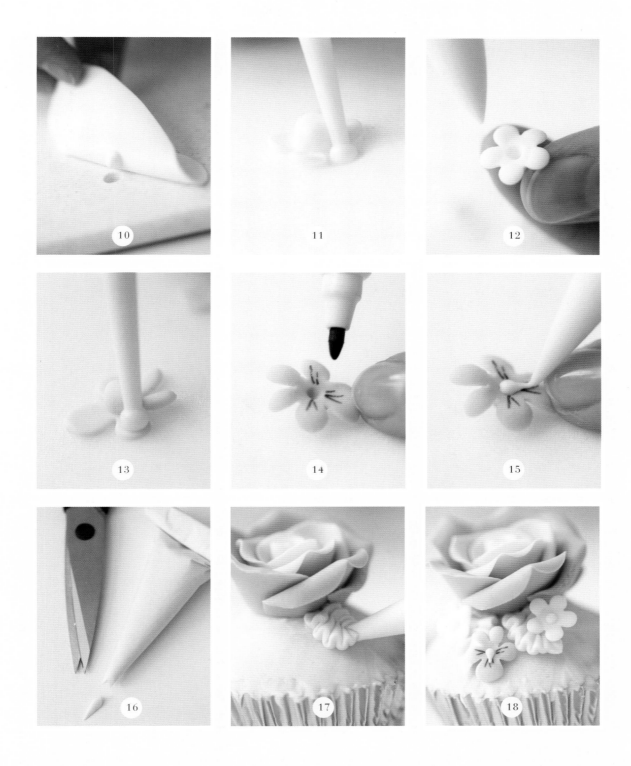

ICELAND POPPIES

NEATLY TAILORED LEMON YELLOW
TIERS SERVE AS THE BACKDROP
FOR THIS ARTFUL ARRANGEMENT
OF CHEERFUL SUGAR POPPIES IN PINK,
CORAL AND YELLOW HUES.

INGREDIENTS

To make 10 small and 10 medium poppies,
plus a few leaves (for miniature cakes only):

About 1kg white flower paste

White vegetable fat

Food paste colour in ivory, primrose, lemon yellow (all from Wilton)
and mint (from Sugarflair)

Petal dust in spring green, primrose, pale terracotta, salmon pink, coral red,
lime zest (all from Rainbow) and tangerine (from Sugarflair)

Pollen dust (from Sugarflair)

Edible glue

10 bunches of small white pointed stamen (1 bunch of stamen makes 2 flower centres)

10 white 22-gauge florist wires, each cut in half

10 white 24gauge florist wires, each cut in half

40 white 28-gauge florist wires, each cut into thirds

1 white 26-gauge wire, cut into thirds (for miniature cakes only)

Cornflour inside a muslin pouch, for dusting

Nile green florist tape, 7mm wide (or 15mm wide, cut in half lengthways)

20 small flower picks

EQUIPMENT

Basic tool kit (see page 11)

Small and medium poppy petal cutters (from Peggy Porschen)

Medium daisy leaf cutter (from Sunflower Sugar Art), for miniature cakes only

Plastic veining board

Poppy petal veiner (from Diamond Paste)

Leaf veiner, for leaves only

Ball tool, for leaves only

Celstick

Tweezers

Wire scissors

Silicone tray with 6cm half-sphere moulds

Polystyrene cake dummy (35cm is ideal for this quantity of poppies)

METHOD

to recreate the cakes For the large cake shown on page 83, you will need a 3-tier stacked cake made up of 3 square tiers measuring 10cm square x 5cm high, 15cm square x 10cm high and 20cm square x 10cm high. All 3 tiers are covered with marzipan and pale yellow sugar paste and are trimmed around the base with a 25mm-wide yellow grosgrain ribbon. The bottom tier sits on a 30cm-square cake drum covered with pale yellow sugar paste and trimmed around the edge with 15mm-wide yellow grosgrain ribbon.

You will also need 3 miniature cakes, 5cm square and 10cm high, covered with marzipan and pale yellow sugar paste and trimmed around the base with 25mm-wide yellow grosgrain ribbon.

You will need 5 poppies in each of the four shades – yellow, peach, pale pink and pink-red.

MAKING THE POPPY CENTRES

Mix 100g of the white flower paste with a small amount of mint and lemon yellow food paste colour to make a light green shade. If the paste feels firm and sticky, add a small dab of vegetable fat, then knead until the paste is smooth and pliable. Wrap in a plastic bag.

Using tweezers, bend one end of each of the 22-gauge florist wires into an open hook.

Shape the green flower paste into 20 small hazelnut-sized balls, about 9mm in diameter.

Take one of the wires and dip the hook end in edible glue, making sure that it is just sticky

and not too wet, then push the hook into a green paste ball (step 1).

Using your tweezers, pinch 8 lines at regular intervals around the top of each poppy centre (step 2). Place them into a polystyrene cake dummy. Repeat until you have 20 balls each on a wire and leave to dry overnight.

Once the poppy centres have dried, lightly brush the paste lines with edible glue and dip them in pollen dust (steps 3–4).

Using tweezers, bend one end of each of the 24-gauge wires into an open hook.

Divide each bunch of stamen in half to make 20 smaller bunches. Gather each bunch in the middle with a wire hook (step 5) and close the wire tightly to hold the stamen in place. Push the stamen upwards on either side of the hook (step 6) and fan them out evenly.

Brush the stamen wires with spring green petal dust and the stamen tips with a blend of primrose and tangerine petal dust (step 7).

Push a wired poppy centre into the middle of the stamen and spread the stamen out evenly around the ball (step 8).

Tape the wires together to make a stem. Wrap the florist tape as far up the stem as possible to hold the stamen and poppy centre tightly in place (step 9). Repeat for the remaining centres.

MAKING THE POPPY PETALS

You will need about 60 small and 60 medium petals in total.

Set aside 50g of white flower paste, then mix the remaining paste with a little primrose and ivory food paste colour to make a pale creamy yellow shade.

Knead the paste until pliable, adding a little white vegetable fat if required. Wrap in a plastic bag and leave to rest for about 15 minutes, until firm.

Roll out some of the paste over a ridge on a plastic veining board. The paste should be no thicker than 1mm, with the vein almost showing through the paste.

Flip the paste over and cut out a petal with a poppy petal cutter – the pointed end should be placed over the thicker end of the vein.

Place the petal on a foam pad and press a Celpin along the rounded edge (step 10).

Dip the tip of a 28-gauge florist wire in edible glue and insert it into the thicker end of the vein, a third of the way into the petal (step 11).

Press the petal in the poppy petal veiner (step 12).

Lightly dust the smooth part of the plastic board with cornflour and lay the petal on top. Frill the rounded edge of the petal using a Celstick (step 13).

Gently bend the florist wire at the base of the petal upwards and place the petal in a half-sphere mould dusted with cornflour (step 14). Repeat for the remaining petals and leave them to dry overnight.

WHITE ROSE & PETALS

THIS TIMELESSLY ELEGANT WEDDING
CAKE REPRESENTS ENDURING GRACE
AND BEAUTY. ONE HUNDRED WHITE ROSE
PETALS, SYMBOLISING PURITY, UNITY
AND TRUE LOVE, FALL FOUR TIERS FROM
A CROWNING HAND-CRAFTED ROSE.

INGREDIENTS

To make 1 large rose and 100 rose petals:

About 600g white flower paste

White vegetable fat

One large polystyrene bud (I use one from Celbud)

About 100g royal icing, stiff-peak consistency (see pages 216–17)

EQUIPMENT

Basic tool kit (see page 11)

Medium and large rose petal cutters (from Peggy Porschen)

Rose petal veiner

Fine craft scissors

2 silicone trays with 4cm half-sphere moulds

Large paper cupcake case

Polystyrene cake dummy

Plastic piping bag

to recreate the cake you will need a 4-tier stacked cake made up of 4 round tiers measuring 10cm (top tier), 15cm (second tier), 20cm (third tier) and 25cm (bottom tier). All 4 tiers are 10cm high and are covered with marzipan and white sugar paste. The bottom tier sits on a 35cm-diameter round cake drum covered with white sugar paste and trimmed around the edge with 15mm-wide white satin ribbon.

Push a cocktail stick into the bottom of the polystyrene bud, making sure it is centred.

Mix the white flower paste with a dab of vegetable fat and knead together until the paste becomes smooth and pliable. Keep inside a sealable plastic bag to prevent it drying out.

Roll out some of the paste to a thickness of about 1mm thick.

Cut out a petal using the medium rose petal cutter. (If in doubt about which size of cutter to use, hold the cutter with the rounded edge against the polystyrene bud. The cutter should just fit over the bud.)

Place the petal on a foam pad and ball with a Celpin (step 1). The edges should become slightly wavy.

Turn the petal over and brush a thin layer of edible glue over the top.

Lay the petal over the polystyrene bud with the rounded side at the top. The tip of the bud should sit centred about 5mm below the top edge of the petal (step 2).

Fold the left petal edge over the tip of the bud, followed by the right edge, then pinch together at the top (step 3). The petal should be closed above the polystyrene bud tip, with the edge that was folded last left slightly open.

Make another 3 petals of the same size; brush only the base of each petal with glue, in a 'V' shape, gluing two-thirds of the way up the left edge and halfway up the right edge of each petal (step 4).

Before gluing on the first petal of the second layer, brush the polystyrene bud exposed below the edge of the previous petal with edible glue (step 5).

Lay the bud over the petal with the point where the glued petals overlap in the centre; the tip of the bud should be about 5mm below the petal edge (step 6). Fold down the left edge of the petal and leave the right side open (step 7).

Turning the bud clockwise, stick the second petal halfway over the first, fold down the left side of the petal and leave the right side open.

Add the third petal so that it half overlaps the second one, and tuck the opposite edge underneath the first petal (step 8). Make sure that all three petals are spaced out evenly and are level at the top.

Using a cocktail stick, fold back the open edge on the right-hand side of each petal (step 9).

The best way to do this is to hold the petal edge with your finger as you wrap and pull the paste around the cocktail stick. Keep the stick parallel to the tip of the bud to maintain the cone shape. Otherwise, the rose will open up too much.

Once you have folded back the right edge of each petal, carefully fold back each left edge. Make sure you don't poke a hole in the paste with the cocktail stick. Gently pinch the top of each petal into a soft tip.

For the next layer, make another 5 petals using the same-size cutter as for the first layer.

After you have balled the petals and before you brush them with edible glue and attach them to the bud, fold back the sides and the top of each petal with a cocktail stick (step 10), following the same technique as for the previous layer. Gently pinch the corners.

Again, brush a 'V' shape of glue onto the base of each petal. Attach the first petal by laying it over the overlap of 2 petals in the previous layer. The petal should sit at the same height as those underneath.

Arrange the remaining 4 petals in the same way as for the previous layer (step 11). Leave to dry, ideally overnight.

Meanwhile, using the medium petal cutter, make about 80 loose petals in the same way as before. Lightly dust the wells of the paint palettes and half-sphere moulds with cornflour and lay the petals in the wells. Leave to dry. They should set within 2 hours.

For the next layer of petals, roll out some more white flower paste and cut out 7 petals using the large petal cutter.

Ball each petal with the Celpin (see page 217) and emboss with the rose petal veiner (step 12).

Fold back the petal edges (step 13), then place them in a paint palette with the folded edges overhanging and the petal tips sitting curved inside the well to create a cup shape (step 14). Let the petals set a little, until they feel leathery.

Once the 7 petals have set, brush edible glue onto the pointed end of each petal in a 'V' shape.

Arrange the first petal over the point where 2 petals overlap, placing it slightly lower than the previous layer.

Turn the rose over and attach the remaining 6 petals from underneath, interlocking them in the same way as with the other layers (step 15).

Once all 7 petals are attached, check that the rose looks even from the top and adjust some of the petals if necessary (step 16).

Place the rose upside down on a soft surface, such as a polystyrene cake dummy, and leave to dry for about 30 minutes (step 17).

Meanwhile, make another 9 petals for the final layer. Snip a couple of tiny wedges into the round edges, close to where the folds will be (step 18).

Ball the petals using the Celpin (step 19).

Lightly dust 9 half-sphere moulds with cornflour and lay the petals with the edges overhanging so the petals curl (step 20) – they should be more open than the petals in the previous layer. Leave to dry.

Meanwhile, make a few more loose petals using the large petal cutter and following the technique in steps 18–20.

Apply the final layer of 9 large petals to the rose (step 21–22), and arrange this petal layer as low as possible, so that the bases touch the cocktail stick.

As before, leave the rose to dry upside down for about 15 minutes, then turn it over and put it in a paper cupcake case (step 23). This will enable the petals to open up slightly without falling off. Place the rose on a polystyrene cake dummy to dry completely (step 24).

To decorate the cake, stick the rose onto the top tier with royal icing. It should tilt forward slightly with the cocktail stick pushed into the cake to hold the rose securely in place. Build up the rose from behind using loose petals, until it is full and has no gaps.

Using royal icing, attach the remaining rose petals randomly all over the cake tiers and scattered across the cake board.

SWEETPEA POSY

MAKE AN IMPACT WITH THESE
ABUNDANT SUGAR FLOWERS.
A BOUQUET OF SWEETPEAS IN
DIFFERENT SIZES AND SHADES IS THE
PERFECT TOPPER FOR ANY CELEBRATION
CAKE. IT CAN BE PRESERVED
AND CHERISHED LONG AFTER
THE CAKE HAS GONE.

INGREDIENTS

To make a posy of 5 long and 3 short sweetpea stems:

About 600g white flower paste

White vegetable fat

Food paste colour in grape violet and gooseberry (both from Sugarflair)
and violet (from Wilton)

Petal dust in mauve and citrus green (from Rainbow)
and lavender and aubergine (both from Sugarflair)

Edible glue

21 green 26-gauge florist wires, cut into 4 even pieces

8 green 2-gauge florist wires

Nile green florist tape

50mm-wide lavender satin ribbon

EQUIPMENT

Basic tool kit (see page 11)

Small rose petal cutter (from Peggy Porschen)

3-piece sweetpea cutter set (from Peggy Porschen)

Tiny calyx cutter (from Peggy Porschen)

Veining tool

Bone tool

Frilling cone tool

Wire scissors

Fine artist's paintbrush

Perforated foam mat

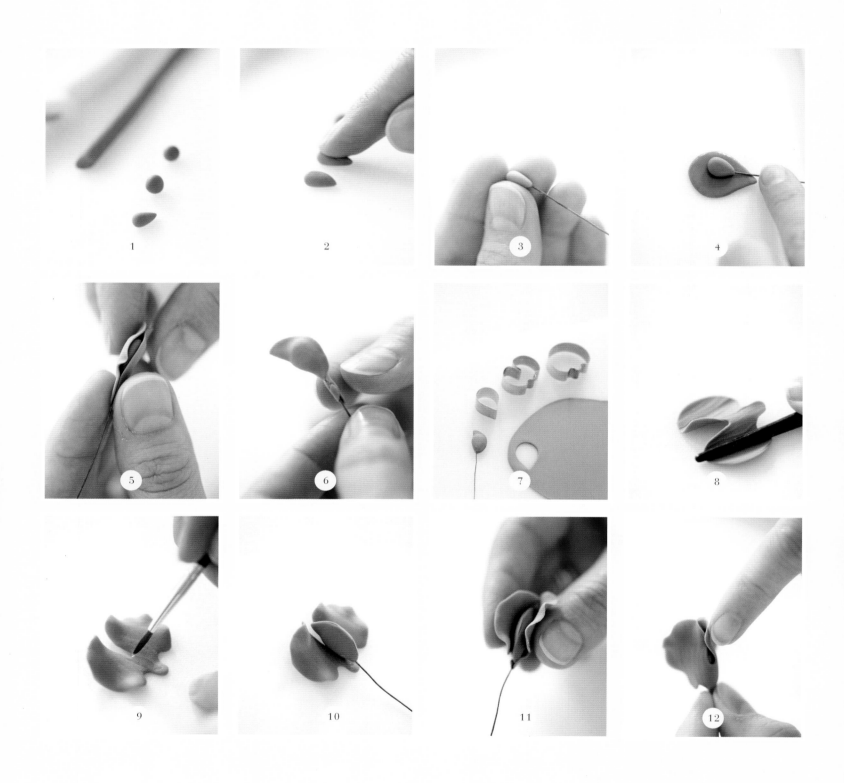

to recreate the cake you will need a round cake measuring 15cm in diameter and 10cm high. The cake is covered with marzipan and white sugar paste and sits on a 20cm-diameter round cake drum covered with white sugar paste and trimmed around the edge with 15mm-wide bridal white satin ribbon.

You can vary the number of blossoms for each stem; however, as a guide, for 1 small stem I made: 2 large dark purple blossoms; 2 medium lavender blossoms; 1 small mauve blossom and 1 mauve bud; and 1 twist. For 1 large stem I made: 3 large dark purple blossoms; 3 medium lavender blossoms; 1 small mauve blossom and 1 mauve bud; and 2 twists.

Begin by mixing the paste colours, starting with the darkest shade, as this will require the longest resting time.

Mix 200g of the white flower paste with enough grape violet food paste colour to make a dark purple shade; the paste will darken further when resting. Knead the paste until it feels smooth and pliable, adding a dab of white vegetable fat, if necessary.

Wrap the paste in a plastic bag and let it rest for at least 15 minutes.

Mix 250g of white flower paste with violet food paste colour to make a lavender shade, and mix 120g of white flower paste with grape violet to make a pale mauve shade. Mix the remaining 30g of white flower paste with gooseberry food paste colour to make a pale green shade.

MAKING THE SWEETPEA CENTRES

You will need about 21 dark purple, 21 lavender and 16 mauve centres. Starting with the dark purple, shape a small amount of paste into a thin sausage about 5mm thick. Cut it into 21 small pieces (step 1) and seal them in a plastic bag to prevent them drying out. Take 1 piece of paste at a time and roll it into a pea-sized ball about 4mm in diameter.

Shape each ball into a teardrop and flatten slightly (step 2). If the pieces are the correct size, they should fit into one half of the rose petal cutter.

Dip the end of a 26-gauge wire in edible glue and push it into the pointed end of the teardrop (step 3). Repeat for the remaining teardrops and let them dry overnight.

MAKING THE SWEETPEA BUDS

Roll out some dark purple paste to a thickness of about 1mm. Cut out a petal using the rose petal cutter and place it on a foam mat.

Ball the petal using the Celpin, until the edges curl up slightly and the paste is slightly stretched. The petal should be large enough to enclose the bud completely.

Brush the surface of the petal with edible glue and place the bud on one half of the petal with the wire towards the petal tip (step 4).

Fold the petal over the bud and gently pinch the edges together so it is enclosed, but showing slightly on one side (step 5). Pinch the excess paste off the bottom (step 6) and leave the bud to dry.

Repeat for the remaining buds using a matching paste colour each time.

MAKING SMALL SWEETPEAS

Roll out some paste in all shades – each blossom must be the same colour as its bud – and cut out 1 petal per flower (plus 8 for the mauve buds) using split sweetpea petal cutter (step 7).

Place a petal on a foam mat and ball it with the Celpin.

Roll the veining tool across the petal, with the pointed end towards the bottom (step 8).

Create wavy edges by running the bone tool back and forth along the petal edge.

Flip the petal over and brush a thin strip of edible glue down the centre (step 9).

Place a wired bud – smooth edge down – on top of the petal (step 10).

Fold the sides up around the bud (step 11).

Add a little more glue at the back and overlap the petal halves (step 12).

Pinch the excess paste off the base of the sweetpea and leave it on a soft surface to dry. Repeat for the remaining sweetpeas.

MAKING MEDIUM SWEETPEAS

Roll out the remaining lavender paste to a thickness of just under 1mm.

Cut out 1 petal per flower using the rounded sweetpea petal cutter.

Place the petal on a foam pad, ball it with a Celpin (step 13) and roll the veining stick across it to emboss.

Create wavy edges with a bone tool (step 14), then brush the petal centre with edible glue. Place a small sweetpea on top and push the sides up slightly, leaving them more open this time.

Pinch off the excess paste at the base (step 15) and place it on a perforated foam mat to dry overnight. Repeat for the remaining medium lavender sweetpeas.

MAKING LARGE SWEETPEAS

Repeat the process applied to make the medium blossoms, but using dark purple paste and flowers. This time, roll out the paste a little thicker and stretch the petals a little more so the finished blossoms are slightly larger than the medium ones.

DUSTING THE SWEETPEAS

Dust the edges with petal dust, brushing each petal from the outside towards the middle (step 16). For the dark purple sweetpeas use aubergine petal dust mixed with a little lavender. For the lavender flowers use the same shades but lighten it with a little more lavender. For the mauve blossoms and buds use mauve petal dust. Brush the large blossoms more heavily than the small ones and only lightly dust the buds.

MAKING THE CALYXES

Once all the flowers have been dusted, roll out the pale green paste until very thin, with a suitably sized Mexican hat (step 17). Cut out 1 calyx per bud and flower (step 18) using the tiny calyx cutter.

Push a frilling cone tool into the middle of each calyx to indent the Mexican hat and brush it with a tiny dab of glue.

Take a wired sweetpea and push the calyx up the wire, sticking it tightly to the base of the flower (step 19). You may need a little more glue to stick down the little calyx petals.

Repeat for the remaining sweetpea blossoms and buds and leave to dry for at least 2 hours.

TAPING THE STEMS TOGETHER

Wrap green florist tape around each wire, from the top to about one-third of the way down (step 20).

To make the twists, tape up the remaining 26-gauge wires (step 21) and go over one end by about 5cm. Tape back the other way, twisting the tape together. Wrap the overlapping tape around a thin paintbrush to curl it.

To create a large stem, take a 22-gauge wire and tape a twist to the end, bringing the tape down to about 2.5cm below the end of the wire.

Add a bud and tape it tightly to the stem, exposing about 1cm of the taped wire.

Continue taping down the stem, adding a small blossom, followed by 3 medium and 3 large flowers, each placed on the opposite side and about 2.5cm lower than the preceding one (steps 22–4). Add 2 twists per stem in between the blossoms, 1 near the upper half and 1 nearer the lower half.

Continue to tape down the wire as far as possible to create a thick long stem, then trim off the ends with wire scissors.

Repeat for the remaining 4 large stems. To make the 3 smaller stems, follow the same technique using 1 bud, 1 small, 2 medium and 2 large blossoms, and 1 twist for each stem.

STEAMING THE SWEETPEAS

Once all the sprays are completed, steam them for about 3 seconds to set the colours. Let them dry for a few minutes, then place on a soft surface until needed.

TO MAKE THE POSY

Gather the sweetpeas at the bottom of the stems and tie them with the 50mm-wide satin ribbon. Make a bow and trim off the ends neatly.

Drape the posy over the top of the cake and bend the blossoms and buds into shape, using tweezers if necessary.

ENGLISH GARDEN ROSES

INSPIRED BY DAVID AUSTIN'S
KEIRA ROSE, THIS UNIQUE BLOOM IS
MADE WITH FOUR CENTRAL
PETAL SECTIONS THAT UNFOLD LAYER
UPON LAYER, ULTIMATELY FORMING
A FULL ROUND ROSE.

INGREDIENTS

To make 1 David Austin-style English rose, 1 large, 1 medium and 1 small rosebud and 4 sets of leaves:

About 500g white flower paste

White vegetable fat

Food paste colour in ivory, pink terracotta (both from Wilton)
and gooseberry (from Sugarflair)

Petal dust in pink candy, light teal and citrus green (all from Rainbow)

Edible glue

4 white 24-gauge florist wires

3 white 26-gauge florist wires, each cut into thirds

White florist tape

3 size 2 polystyrene buds (I used Celbuds)

Cornflour in a small muslin pouch, for dusting

Selection of small plastic flower picks

Small amount of royal icing

Pearl spray (from PME)

EQUIPMENT

Basic tool kit (see page 11)

Small, medium and large rose petal cutter (from Peggy Porschen)

Medium and large calyx cutters (from Peggy Porschen)

Large and medium rose leaf cutters (from Peggy Porschen)

Silicone rose petal veiner

Silicone rose leaf veiner

Small thin rolling pin

Tweezers

Bone tool

Dresden tool or veining tool

Wire scissors

Flat wide artist's paintbrush

Silicone tray with 6cm half-sphere moulds or supermarket polystyrene apple tray

Polystyrene cake dummy

Mug with clingfilm stretched over the top

Kitchen paper

Small circular cutter set (from PME)

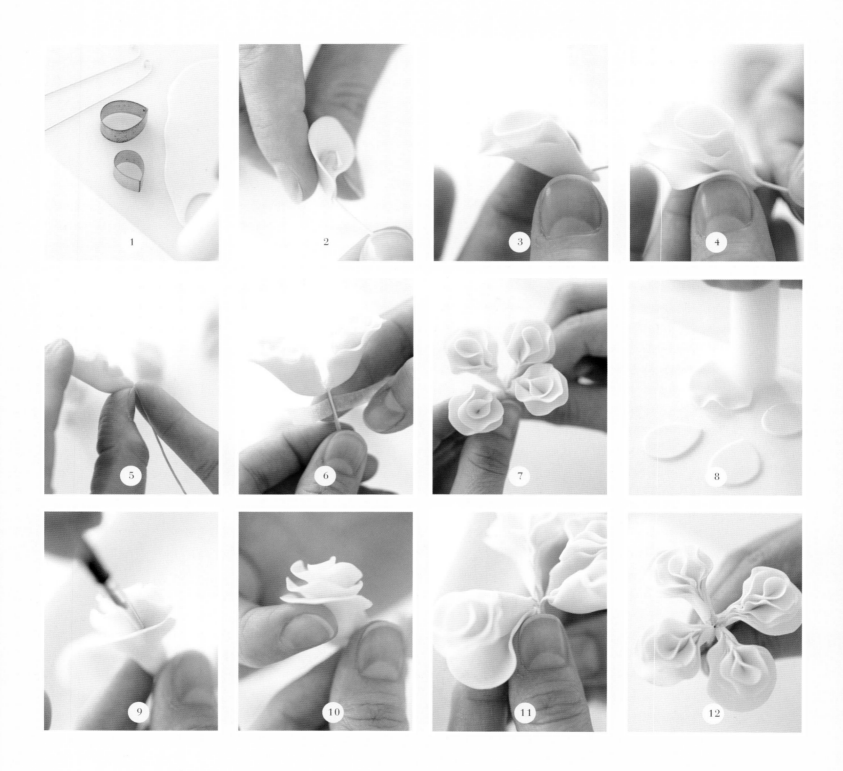

METHOD

to recreate the cake you will need a stacked 2-tier round cake measuring: 10cm in diameter and 5cm high (top tier); and 15cm in diameter and 15cm high (bottom tier). Both tiers are covered with marzipan and ivory sugar paste. The bottom tier sits on a 20cm-diameter round cake drum covered with ivory sugar paste and trimmed around the edge with 15mm-wide bridal white satin ribbon.

The sides of the cake tiers are decorated with cut-out dots made from equal quantities of flower and sugar pastes, mixed together and coloured with pink terracotta, peach and lemon yellow food colour (from Wilton). The dots have been shimmered with pearl spray (from PME) before being attached to the cake with edible glue.

Mix about 400g of white flower paste with a dab of white vegetable fat and knead until the paste feels smooth and pliable.

Take about one-third of the paste and add a small amount of pink terracotta food paste colour and mix to make a pale pink shade.

Mix the remaining two-thirds of the paste with ivory food colour to make a pale ivory shade.

Wrap the paste in plastic bags and leave to rest for about 15 minutes until firm.

MAKING THE ROSE CENTRE
The rose centre is formed of 4 individually wired sets of petals, which will be merged together to form a cross-shaped bud.

Cut 1 of the 24-gauge wires into 4 even pieces.

Bend 1 end of each wire to make a curved hook, using a small rolling pin and tweezers. Ensure that all 4 hooks are roughly the same size and shape.

Roll out the pink flower paste until very thin, then cut out 1 small petal for each hooked wire (step 1). Place the rose petals on a foam pad and ball them with a Celpin.

Flip the petals over and brush the bottom half with glue.

Fold the bottom half of each petal over a hook and squeeze the sides together, leaving the upper part open (step 2). Ensure the hook is not showing on the inside of the petal.

Let all 4 petals dry overnight.

Once dry, make another 4 petals in the same way, but this time roll out the paste slightly thicker and stretch the petals out further with the Celpin, to make them a little larger than the first petals.

Brush glue onto the bottom part of a dry wired petal and fold a fresh petal around it (step 3). Make sure the petal closes cleanly over the wired base of the previous petal and opens up and out at the top. Repeat for the remaining 3 petals.

Gradually mix the remaining pink paste with a little ivory paste to make a lighter pink. Use this paste to make another 4 petals using the medium rose petal cutter.

After balling (see page 219), use a bone tool to create wavy edges, then glue each petal over a petal from the previous layer (step 4).

Let the petals set for 2 hours or ideally overnight.

Once dry, carefully bend the petals back (step 5) and tape all 4 centres together to make a cross shape (steps 6–7).

Set aside about 50g of the remaining pink paste, then add to the rest a little more ivory paste. Make another 4 petals using the medium cutter. These petals should be stretched out a little further than those made earlier (step 8).

Before you glue on the petals (step 9), bend out the 4 petal centres so there is enough space for your fingers to wrap a petal around each one (step 10). For a neat finish, be as clean as possible. Each petal needs to completely cover the lower front of the previous petal to cover the wire (step 11).

Make another 8 petals using the large rose petal cutter. Repeat the process followed for the last layer, to add another 2 layers (step 12).

While the petals are still soft, push all 4 centres back up until they meet in the middle (step 13). Gently squeeze the paste together to hide any wires that might be visible at the bottom.

Take the half-sphere silicone tray (I poked a hole in the middle of one of the spheres using a cork screw) and place the rose centre in one of the wells to dry overnight.

MAKING THE OUTER PETALS

Once the rose centre is dry, roll out the ivory paste to a thickness of about 1mm.

Cut out about 8 petals for the next layer using the large rose petal cutter.

Place the petals on a foam pad and ball the edges with a Celpin.

Press each petal in a rose petal veiner.

Place the petals back on the foam pad and frill the edges with a bone tool.

Dust the silicon sphere moulds lightly with cornflour and lay a petal in each mould. Leave to set until they feel leathery.

While the petals are still flexible, brush a 'V' shape of edible glue on the bottom of each one (step 14).

Arrange the petals around the rose centre (steps 15–17). The outer edge of the petals should cup the centre and the sides of the petals should overlap by about half. The last petal should be half over and half under the previous two. You may find it easier to attach the petals if you hold your rose centre upside down. Leave the petals to set for 30 minutes.

Meanwhile, make another 8–10 petals, in the same way as for the previous layer.

Make a few tiny snips in the petal edges using scissors or the tip of a small rose petal cutter. Ball the petals, stretching them slightly, to make each one a little larger than those of the previous layer. Attach the petals all around as before (steps 18–19).

Place the rose over the clingfilm-covered mug and support the outer petals with rolled-up strips of kitchen paper. Let the petals dry overnight in a cupped, yet open, shape (see page 180, step 8).

MAKING THE ROSEBUDS

You will need 1 closed, 1 half-open and 1 open rosebud.

Push a cocktail stick through the base of each polystyrene bud, from one side to the other, to create a tunnel.

Push a 24-gauge wire through each tunnel and bend the wire around the base on each side.

Bend the two ends in the middle and twist together tightly to form a stem. Make sure there is no gap between the bud and the wire, otherwise your petals will not attach properly.

TO MAKE THE CLOSED ROSEBUDS

To make the first petal for each rosebud, roll out the remaining pink paste to a thickness of about 1mm and cut out 3 small petals using the smallest petal cutter.

Place the petals on the foam pad and ball them using the Celpin (step 20). Then flip each one over.

Brush the petals with a thin layer of edible glue. Place a polystyrene bud on top of a petal with the tip of the bud centred towards the rounded side of the petal, about 5mm below the petal edge (step 21).

Fold the petal over the tip of the polystyrene bud from the left, pinch the top of the petal to close the tip, then fold the right side of the petal over. Ensure that the tip is covered (step 22). Repeat for the remaining petals.

Add some ivory paste to the remaining pink paste to lighten it slightly, then make another 9 small petals as above. Use the bone tool to make wavy edges.

Brush a 'V' of edible glue onto the bottom half of each petal.

Take 1 rosebud and arrange 3 petals around the first petal, overlapping them by about half (steps 23–4). All the petals should sit at the same height, a few millimeters above the first petal. Ensure that there is no polystyrene showing inside the rose.

Curl out the petal edges slightly with your fingers (step 25).

Repeat for the remaining buds and let them set on a polystyrene cake dummy.

TO MAKE THE HALF-OPEN AND OPEN ROSEBUDS

Roll out a small amount of ivory flower paste and cut out 3 medium petals for the half-open and 5 for the open rosebud.

This time, frill the petal edges a little more and keep the petals slightly more open when sticking them on (step 26). Repeat for the remaining buds and let them set.

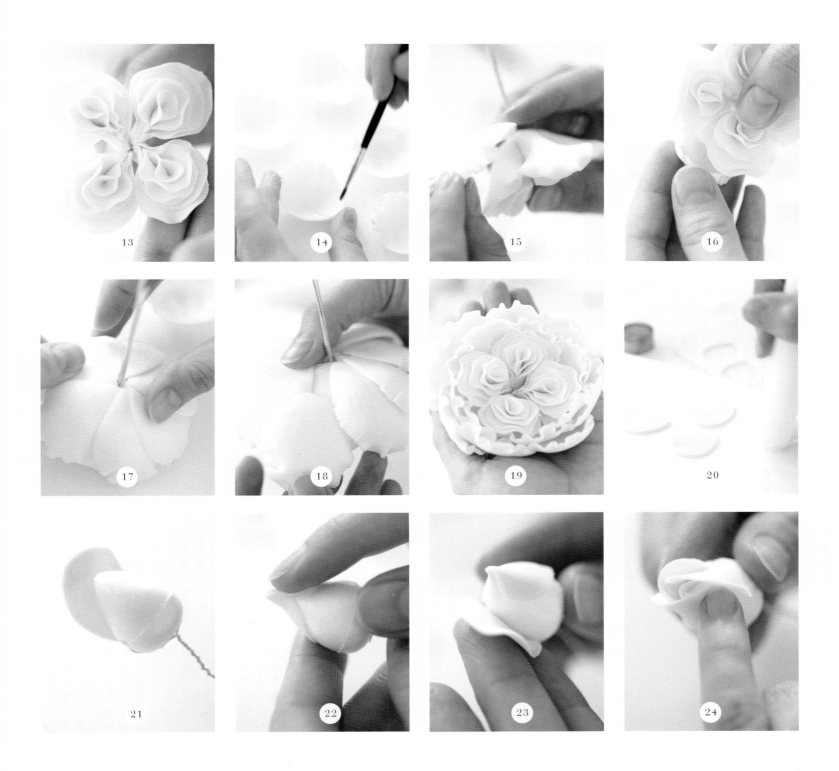

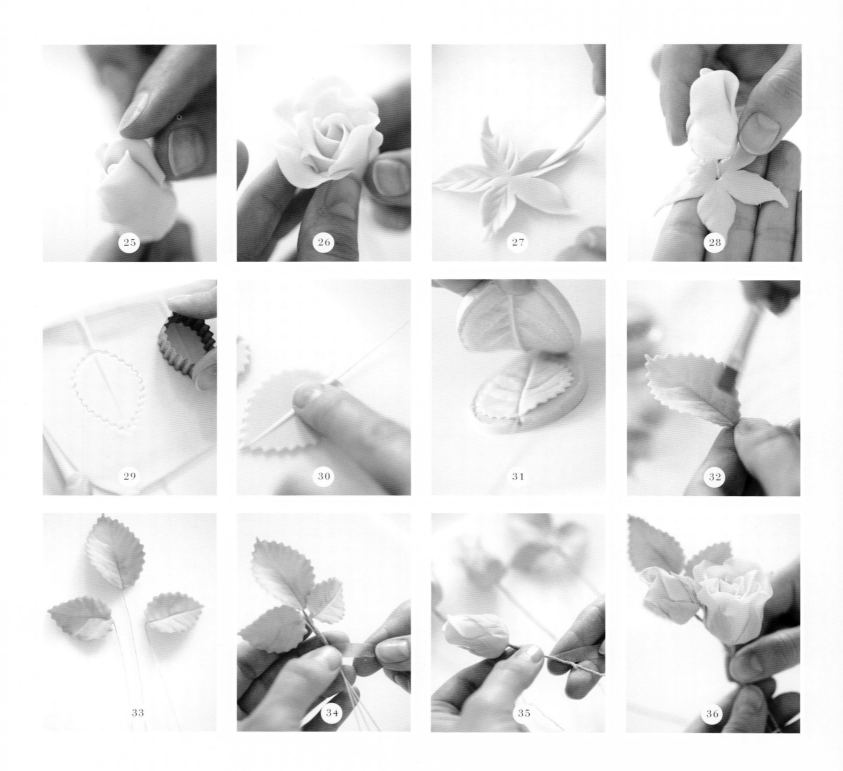

MAKING THE CALYXES

Mix 100g of white flower paste with a small amount of vegetable fat and knead until smooth and pliable.

Add a small amount of gooseberry food paste colour and mix to make a pale green shade.

Wrap the paste in a plastic bag and leave to rest for about 15 minutes.

Roll out the paste thinly and, using the calyx cutters, cut out 3 medium calyxes for the rosebuds and 1 large one for the large rose.

Slightly widen the calyx petals with a Celpin and thin the edges.

Using the thin end of a Dresden tool, emboss leaf veins into each calyx petal (step 27).

Flip each calyx over and brush thinly with edible glue.

Lay 1 medium calyx flat in your hand, glue side up, and stick the wire of a rosebud through the middle (step 28). Push it all the way down until the base of the bud sits in the middle of the calyx, then bring the petals up against the sides, covering any visible parts of the polystyrene bud. Repeat for the remaining buds and the rose.

MAKING THE LEAVES

You will need 3 sets of leaves, each made up of 1 large and 2 medium leaves. Roll out the remaining green flower paste thinly, using a veining board to create pencil veins.

Place a leaf cutter centred over a vein, with the thicker end going through the base and the thinner end at the tip of the leaf (step 29). Cut out 3 large and 6 medium leaves

Place a leaf on a foam pad and dip a 26-gauge wire in glue. Push the wire about one-third of the way into the vein from the base (step 30).

Use a Celpin to thin the leaf edges and flatten the pencil vein.

Press the leaf in a rose leaf veiner (step 31) and place it, curved, on a perforated foam mat. Repeat for the remaining leaves and allow them to dry overnight.

DUSTING THE ROSES

Dust the edges of the rose and rosebud petals with pink candy petal dust, using the flat wide artist's paintbrush.

Dust the leaves with a mixture of citrus green and light teal petal dust. Brush from the bottom of each leaf upwards, and from the edges towards the centre (step 32).

TAPING THE ROSES AND LEAVES TOGETHER

Take the large leaves and wrap green florist tape around the top 1cm of each wire.

Sharply bend the wires of the medium leaves to the side, to an angle of 90°; 3 of the leaves should bend to the right and 3 to the left (step 33).

Take a large leaf and hold 2 medium leaves, one on either side, at the same height. Tape them around the wire of the large leaf (step 34). Repeat to complete all 3 sets of leaves.

Tape the stem of each rosebud down by a few centimetres (step 35), then tape together 1 small and 1 large bud and leaves (step 36).

STEAMING THE ROSES

Steam the roses for about 3 seconds to set the colour. Leave them to dry for a few minutes until the paste is no longer sticky.

ASSEMBLING THE ROSES

Push the wires into flower picks and then into the cake. Use a dab of royal icing at the back of the large rose to hold it in place, if required.

CLIMBING COSMOS

A SIMPLE BUT STUNNING FLOWER
THAT COMES TO LIFE THROUGH
SPLASHES OF COLOUR APPLIED
WITH PETAL DUST. THIS CAKE SEEMS
TO RISE FROM A GARDEN OF
CLIMBING COSMOS.

INGREDIENTS

To make about 20 large, 20 medium and 20 small cosmos:

About 500g white flower paste

White vegetable fat

Food paste colour in claret, spruce green (both from Sugarflair) and primrose (from Wilton)

Petal dust in plum and primrose (from Sugarflair)

Cornflour in a small muslin pouch, for dusting

Edible glue

1 tablespoon semolina

About 150g royal icing, soft-peak consistency (see pages 216–17)

EQUIPMENT

Basic tool kit (see page 11)

Fantasy flower cutter set of 3 (from Stephen Benison)

Flower centre mould (from Diamond Paste)

Shell tool

Flat wide artist's paintbrush

1 silicone tray with 4cm half-sphere moulds

2 silicone trays with 6cm half-sphere moulds

2 paper piping bags

METHOD

to recreate the cake you will need a stacked 3-tier round cake measuring 10cm, 15cm and 20cm in diameter, and all 10cm high. All tiers are covered with marzipan and white sugar paste. The bottom tier sits on a 30cm-diameter round cake drum covered with white sugar paste and trimmed around the edge with 15mm-wide bridal white satin ribbon.

The miniature cakes are round (5cm-diameter x 5cm high) sponge cakes covered with marzipan and white sugar paste.

Mix 400g of the white flower paste with a small amount of claret food paste colour to make a very pale pink shade. If the paste feels firm and sticky, add a dab of white vegetable fat and knead until the paste is smooth and pliable.

Roll out some of the paste to a thickness of about 1mm, then cut out a few flower shapes at a time using the fantasy flower cutter (step 1). You will need a total of about 20 large, 20 medium and 20 small flowers.

Place a flower shape on a foam pad and ball the centre and the petal edges with a Celpin (step 2).

Run the shell tool from each petal edge towards the flower centre using sufficient pressure to make the petal curl up (step 3).

Lay the flower in the well of a half-sphere mould that has been lightly dusted with cornflour (step 4). For the large flowers use a 6cm mould, for the medium flowers use a 4cm mould and for the small flowers use the wells in a paint palette.

Repeat for the remaining flowers and leave them to dry overnight.

Mix the remaining flower paste with primrose food paste colour and make about 60 pea-sized ball shapes.

Push each ball into the fourth-largest well of the flower centre mould (steps 5–6).

Once the flowers are dry, brush the petal edges with plum petal dust using a flat wide artist's paintbrush (step 7). Follow the lines on each petal to enhance them. The colour should gradually become lighter towards the centre.

Brush the middle of each flower with edible glue and stick the ball shapes in place, to make the flower centres (step 8).

Mix the semolina with a small amount of primrose petal dust (step 9).

Brush the yellow flower centres with edible glue and sprinkle the semolina over the top to cover completely. Tip off the excess semolina (step 10).

Mix the royal icing with spruce green food paste colour and transfer to a piping bag.

Snip off the tip and pipe stems down the sides of the miniature cakes and cake tiers – vary the heights of the stems. Tilt the cakes away from you slightly as you pipe, to help prevent the icing from drooping.

To add some small leaves, pipe a dot, then drag it towards the stem (step 11).

Pipe a blob of icing at the top of each stem and attach a cosmos flower (step 12). Hold the flower against the side for a few seconds, to help the icing set. If the weight of the flowers pulls the stems down, add a little icing sugar to your royal icing to stiffen it.

PEONIES

IN VARIOUS STATES OF BLOOM,
A SUMMERTIME DISPLAY OF PEONIES
FLOATS ON A SINGLE-TIER CAKE.
PEONIES REPRESENT PROSPERITY,
GOOD HEALTH AND MARITAL HAPPINESS.
THEY ARE IN FULL BLOOM IN EARLY
SUMMER, SO PEONIES ARE AN
IDEAL CHOICE FOR WEDDING CAKES.

INGREDIENTS

To make 3 large, 1 medium and 2 small peonies and 1 bud,
plus the appliqué leaves:

About 500g white flower paste

White vegetable fat

Food paste colour in peach, willow green (both from Wilton) and claret (from Sugarflair)

Petal dust in candy pink and peach (both from Rainbow)

Cornflour in a small muslin pouch, for dusting

Edible glue

7 polystyrene balls, 3cm in diameter

Small amount of royal icing

EQUIPMENT

Basic tool kit (see page 11)

Peony cutter and veiner set (from Petal Crafts)

Large and medium Virginia creeper leaf cutter (from Peggy Porschen)

Medium and small multipurpose leaf cutters (from Peggy Porschen)

4cm and 8cm round pastry cutters

Ball tool

Bone tool

Dresden tool

Fine and flat wide artist's paintbrush

Silicone tray with 4cm half-sphere moulds

Selection of small and large paper cupcake cases

Polystyrene cake dummy

3 mugs with clingfilm stretched over the top

Kitchen paper

Paper piping bag

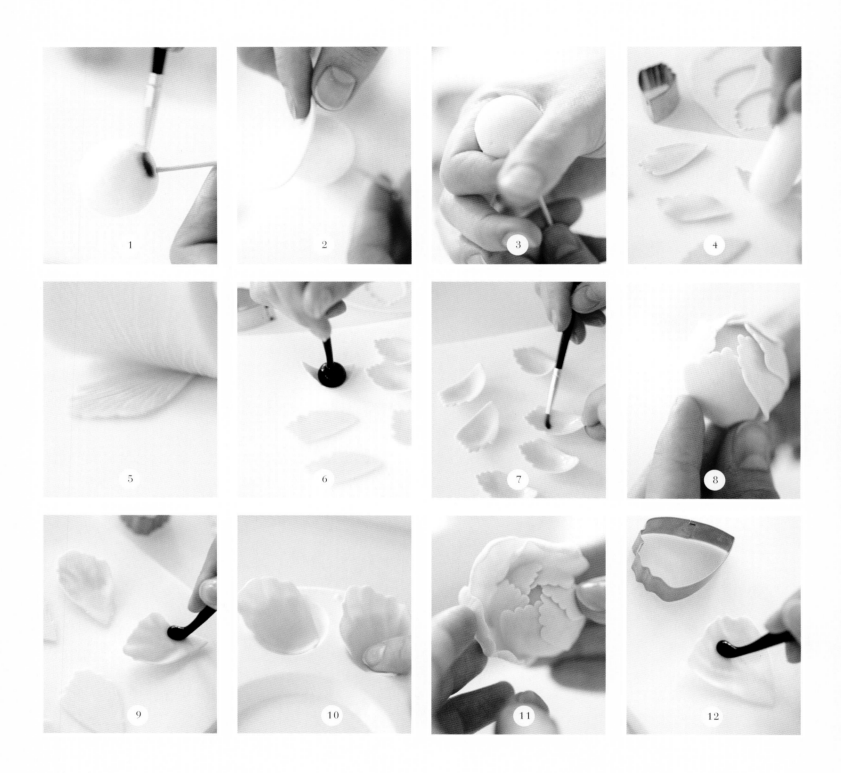

METHOD

to recreate the cake you will need a round cake measuring 15cm in diameter and 12cm high. The cake is covered with marzipan and white sugar paste and is trimmed around the base with a 25mm-wide pink satin ribbon. The cake sits on a 20cm-diameter round cake drum covered with white sugar paste and trimmed around the edge with 15mm-wide pink satin ribbon.

MAKING THE PEONY BUDS

Mix 150g of white flower paste with peach food paste colour and knead it until smooth and pliable. Add a small amount of vegetable fat if the paste feels firm and sticky.

Wrap the paste in a plastic bag or clingfilm and leave to rest for about 15 minutes.

Push a cocktail stick into the centre of each polystyrene ball.

Roll out some of the peach flower paste thinly and cut out a circle for each polystyrene ball using the larger round pastry cutter.

Brush one of the polystyrene balls thinly with edible glue (step 1) and place a circle of paste centred on top (step 2), then gently smooth it down the sides with your fingers (step 3). Don't worry if the paste doesn't cover the ball completely, as long as it is smooth and thin and the upper part of the ball is covered. Repeat for the other 6 polystyrene balls.

For the first layer of petals, roll out another piece of peach paste and cut out 6 petals with the smallest peony petal cutter.

Place them on a foam pad and ball the edges with the Celpin (step 4).

Centre the petal veining mat over each petal and press to emboss veins on the paste (step 5).

Turn the petals over and run a ball tool from the centre of each petal down towards the base, applying enough pressure to make the edges curl up (step 6).

Brush the lower two-thirds of each petal thinly with edible glue (step 7) and arrange them evenly around the ball, overlapping the sides and leaving a small gap at the top (step 8).

Using your hand, flatten the petals around the sides of the bud to maintain a round shape.

Repeat this process for the remaining buds and place them on a polystyrene cake dummy to set.

MAKING THE SMALL PEONIES

Mix 100g of white flower paste with the remaining peach paste and add a few drops of claret food paste colour to make a peachy pink shade. Add some vegetable fat if the paste feels firm and sticky.

Wrap the paste in a plastic bag or clingfilm and leave to rest for about 15 minutes.

Repeat steps 1–5 to make another 6–8 petals per flower (except 1 of them), using the smallest petal cutter.

Turn the petals over and run the thin end of a bone tool from the tip of each petal, along the middle to about halfway, applying enough

pressure to make thick grooves (step 9).

Place each petal in the well of a paint palette dusted with a thin layer of cornflour (step 10), and leave them to set until they feel leathery.

Brush the bottom edges of each petal with a thin layer of edible glue in a 'V' shape, to about halfway up the sides.

Arrange 7–8 petals around each bud, overlapping the sides evenly (step 11), then place the buds in suitably sized paper cupcake cases and leave to dry for about 2 hours.

MAKING THE MEDIUM PEONIES

Repeat the process as for the small peonies, adding 100g of white flower paste to the remaining peachy pink paste and mixing in a little claret food paste colour to make a deeper pink shade. Use the medium petal cutter (step 12). You will need 7–8 petals for 1 flower. Place the petals in the wells of a half-sphere tray dusted with cornflour (step 13–14), and, once assembled and placed in cupcake cases, let the peonies dry overnight.

MAKING THE LARGE PEONIES

Repeat the process, adding 100g of white flower paste and a little claret food paste colour. Use the large petal cutter to make 8 petals for the outer layer of the 3 flowers. You may find it easier to arrange the petals while holding the flower upside down (step 15); this will help prevent the petals from falling down.

Let the last petal layer set while resting the peonies upside down on a polystyrene cake dummy or foam pad.

Dust the clingfilm-covered mugs with cornflour. Once the peonies are set, turn them over and lay them on the clingfilm to dry overnight. To prevent the petals from closing or opening up too far, roll up some thin strips of kitchen paper and place them in between and around the petals for extra support.

DUSTING THE PEONIES

Brush the peony buds and the centres of the large flowers with peach petal dust (step 16) and the outer petal layers with candy pink, using a flat wide artist's paintbrush. Work from the petal edges downwards and from the inside of the open petals upwards; also brush the backs of the outer petals.

STEAMING THE PEONIES

Steam each peony for about 3 seconds to set the colours and give them a satin-like sheen.

FINISHING THE BUD

Mix about 25g of white flower paste with green food paste colour to make a mint green shade, then roll out the paste until very thin.

Select a small round pastry cutter that fits neatly over the bud (step 17) and cut out 2 circles (step 18) from the green paste.

Place the circles on a foam pad and thin the edges with a Celpin (step 19).

Brush the circles with edible glue and stick them around the sides of the bud so they overlap slightly on one side and are open on the other, revealing the petals at the top (step 20).

Pinch off the excess green paste at the bottom (step 21).

LEAF APPLIQUÉ

Mix about 25g of white flower paste with a dab of white vegetable fat and knead until the paste feels smooth and pliable. Divide the paste in half and add green food paste colour, mixing one half to a very pale green and the other half to a slightly darker shade.

Roll out both pieces of paste to a thickness of about 1mm, or slightly less.

Cut out some leaf shapes (about 5 of each size; you should end up with an even number of leaves) using the Virginia creeper cutters for the darker green paste and the multipurpose cutters for the lighter paste (step 22).

Place the pale green leaves on a foam pad and emboss leaf veins using the Dresden tool (step 23) or the veining tool.

Using edible glue, stick the medium pale green leaves on top of the large dark green leaves, and the small pale green leaves on top of the medium dark green leaves (step 24).

While soft, stick the leaves around the sides and over the edges of the cake.

TO DECORATE THE CAKE

Brush a dab of royal icing onto the backs of the peonies and push the cocktail sticks into the cake.

CHRYSANTHEMUM TREES

MADE USING A SILICONE MOULD,
THIS SEASONAL FLORAL DESIGN
CREATES THE PERFECT
FESTIVE CENTREPIECE WITH
A WOW FACTOR.

INGREDIENTS

To make a small cone cake and about 40 chrysanthemums:

9 round sponge layers: 3 x 10cm-diameter; 3 x 15cm-diameter; 3 x 20cm-diameter

About 2.5kg buttercream

About 300ml sugar syrup

3 round cake drums, 10cm, 15cm and 20cm in diameter

About 2kg marzipan

Icing sugar, for dusting

About 2kg white sugar paste, plus about 250g for the flowers

About 750g white flower paste

White vegetable fat

Food paste colour in red extra, gooseberry (both from Sugarflair)

or moss green (from Wilton)

8 plastic cake dowels

Round cake board, 25cm in diameter

Small amount of vodka

About 150g royal icing

To make a large cone cake and 60 chrysanthemums, you will need an additional:

3 x 25cm-diameter round sponge layers

About 1kg buttercream

About 175ml sugar syrup

About 1kg marzipan

About 1kg white sugar paste, plus about 150g for the flowers

About 450g white flower paste

4 plastic cake dowels

Round cake board, 30cm in diameter

EQUIPMENT

Layering and icing kits (see pages 204 and 209)

Silicone chrysanthemum mould (from First Impressions)

Scissors

Paper piping bag

METHOD

to recreate the cakes you will need the ingredients and equipment listed on page 134.

MAKING THE FLOWERS

Mix together the 250g white sugar paste and white flower paste, adding a small dab of vegetable fat if the paste feels sticky.

Colour the paste in your chosen shade, then leave it rest for about 30 minutes, until firm.

Mix 100g of royal icing with the same food paste colour as you used for the paste and transfer it to a piping bag.

Rub the inside of the silicone chrysanthemum mould with a thin layer of white vegetable fat.

Shape the paste into balls about 12mm in diameter (step 1), then wrap them in a plastic bag to prevent them from drying.

When ready to make the flowers, push a ball of paste firmly into the mould (step 2) and flatten so it is flush with the mould.

Tap the edge of the mould on a hard surface, several times, until the chrysanthemum falls out (steps 3–4).

Repeat to make about 40 chrysanthemums for a small cake or 60 for a large cake.

BUILDING THE CAKES

Layer and mask the sponge cakes (using one cake of each size) with sugar syrup and buttercream, following the instructions given on page 206.

Stack them naked (without a marzipan or sugar paste covering), using the plastic cake dowels, following the instructions given on page 214. Use buttercream instead of royal icing to hold the cake tiers together.

Chill the tiered cakes for about 30 minutes, to set the buttercream in between the tiers.

Meanwhile, mix 2kg sugar paste to the same shade as the flowers for this cake. Wrap the paste with clingfilm to prevent it drying out.

Place the cake on a non-stick turntable and carve the edges into a cone shape by pressing the palette knife against the edges of the drums and using them as a guide (steps 5–6).

Shape a marzipan cone for the tip of the cake and stick it onto the top tier with buttercream.

Place the cake on a disc or drum 5cm larger than the cake base.

Spread a thin layer of buttercream all over the surface of the cake.

On a surface dusted with icing sugar, roll out the marzipan to a thickness of about 5mm and so it is large enough to cover the cone cake (step 7).

Cover the cone cake with the marzipan (step 8), using a large rolling pin to lift it.

Trim off any excess marzipan (step 9) and leave it to set overnight at room temperature.

Brush the marzipan with vodka or cooled boiled water, then roll out the coloured sugar paste to a thickness of about 5mm. Cover the cake with the sugar paste, following the same process as for the marzipan.

Roll out the leftover sugar paste to a thickness of about 3mm, then use it to cover the cake card following the instructions on page 213.

Leave the sugar paste to set overnight.

TO DECORATE THE CAKE

Spread the remaining white royal icing across the centre of the iced cake card and stick the cone cake on top.

Using the royal icing, stick the flowers onto the cake while the paste is still soft and pliable. Start at the bottom of the cone and build up the layers, row by row.

WHITE ORCHIDS

THERE IS SOMETHING SO TIMELESS,
ELEGANT AND SOPHISTICATED ABOUT
WHITE ORCHIDS - THEIR APPEAL NEVER
SEEMS TO FADE. THERE ARE HUNDREDS
OF ORCHIDS TO CHOOSE FROM.
I HAVE SELECTED THREE VARIETIES,
EACH WITH ITS OWN UNIQUE CHARM.

SINGAPORE ORCHID

INGREDIENTS

To make a spray of 6 Singapore orchids and 8 buds:

About 250g white flower paste

White vegetable fat

Food paste colour in gooseberry (from Sugarflair)

Petal dust in citrus green and primrose (from Rainbow)

Edible glue

2 white 24-gauge florist wires, each cut into 3 even pieces

2 white 26-gauge wires, each cut into 4 even pieces

1 white 20-gauge wire

Nile green florist tape

1 plastic flower pick

EQUIPMENT

Basic tool kit (see page 11)

Singapore orchid cutter set (from Peggy Porschen)

Orchid petal veiner (from SK Great Impressions)

Dresden tool

Bone tool

Frilling cone tool

Celstick

Flat wide artist's paintbrush

Wire scissors

Tweezers

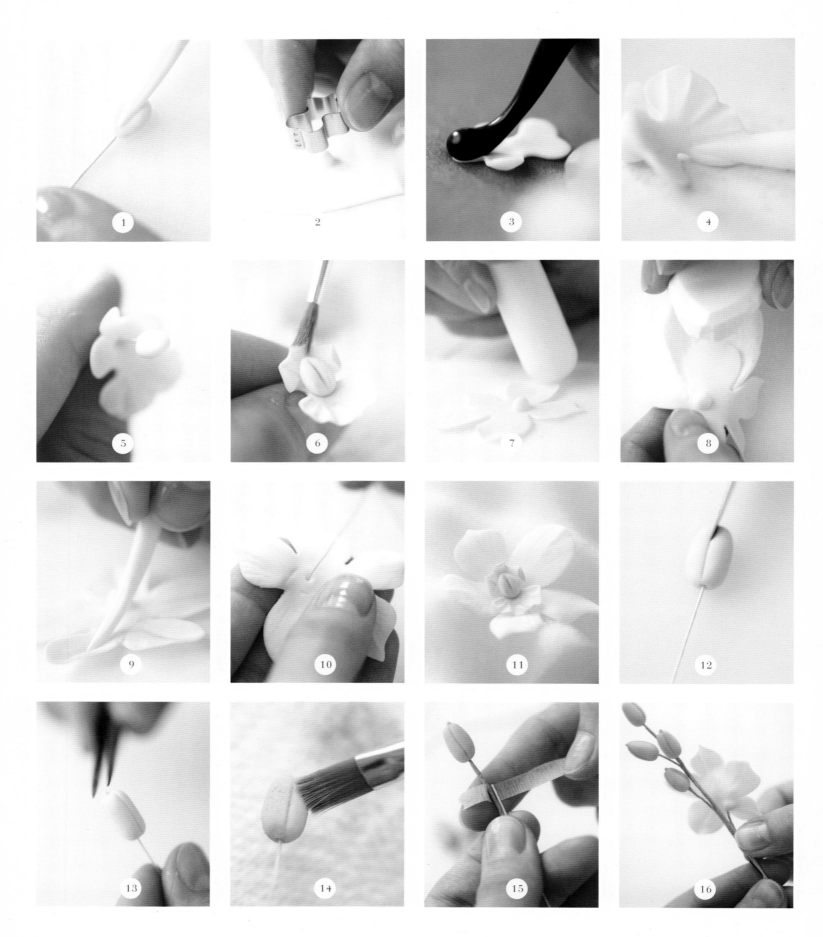

METHOD

to recreate the cake you will need a cake measuring 10cm in each direction, covered with marzipan and pale green sugar paste and trimed around the bottom edge with 15mm-wide lime green satin ribbon. The cake sits on a 15cm-square cake card covered with pale green sugar paste.

Each orchid is made up of a wired pod with a throat attached to it, and a 5-piece petal.

Knead the white flower paste until smooth and pliable. If the paste feels firm and sticky, add a small dab of white vegetable fat. Wrap the paste wrapped in a plastic bag or clingfilm to prevent it from drying out.

MAKING THE SINGAPORE ORCHIDS

To make the pods, using the flower paste, shape 6 small balls with a diameter of about 3mm.

One at a time, place the ball shapes on the palm of your hand and roll into a teardrop. Dip the end of a 24-gauge wire in edible glue and push it halfway into the pointed end of the teardrop.

Place it on a foam pad and score the teardrop down the middle with the thin end of a Dresden tool (step 1).

Repeat for the remaining 5 ball shapes and leave them to dry overnight.

Once dry, make the orchid throats. Roll out some white flower paste on the plastic board, over a suitably sized hole for a Mexican hat.

Select the throat cutter from the orchid cutter set and place it on the paste with the Mexican hat between the 3 smaller petals of the cutter (step 2).

Cut out the throat shape and place it on the foam pad so the Mexican hat sits in a hole.

Using a bone tool, thin out and stretch the 3 smaller parts of the throat (step 3), then run the tool from the edges to the middle to make the edges curl up.

Lightly dust a plastic board with cornflour and place the throat on the board with the Mexican hat facing down. Use a Celstick to frill the edges of the lower part of the throat, to create the lip (step 4).

Hold the throat between your fingers and push a well into the middle of the Mexican hat, using a frilling cone tool.

Guide the wire of a pod into the well from the top (step 5), then brush a little glue around the well and the upper part of the throat. Push the throat up around the pod and leave to dry for a couple of hours.

Repeat this process using the remaining ball shapes, to make another 5 orchid throats.

Once dry, dust the columns and the inner part of the throat with a blend of citrus green and primrose petal dust (step 6).

Roll out some more white flower paste on the plastic board, over the largest Mexican hat. Centre the orchid cutter over the top of the Mexican hat and cut out a flower shape.

Place the shape on the foam pad and ball the petal edges with a Celpin (step 7).

Press each petal in the orchid petal veiner (step 8).

Place the orchid shape back on the foam mat and score the back of each petal with the thin

end of a Dresden tool by moving it from the tip to the centre (step 9).

Flip over the orchid shape and hold it in your hand. Using the frilling cone tool, push a well into the middle of the Mexican hat.

Brush the area around the well with glue and push the wire of the throat through the well from the top (step 10). The lip of the throat should sit centred above the join of the 2 pointed petals (step 11).

Push the orchid wire through the well of a perforated foam mat and place the mat over a bowl or plastic container to allow room for the wire underneath. Leave the orchid to dry overnight.

Repeat the process for the remaining 5 orchids.

MAKING THE BUDS

Mix the remaining white flower paste with gooseberry food paste colour, then make 8 ball shapes about 6mm in diameter. Shape into oval buds.

Dip the end of a 26-gauge wire in glue and push it halfway into the bud, lengthways.

Using a kitchen knife, score the sides of the bud to make 4 equal sections (step 12).

Pinch the top of the bud into a small tip using tweezers (step 13).

Repeat to make the remaining 7 buds and leave them to dry overnight.

Once dry, brush the buds all over with citrus green petal dust (step 14).

Continued overleaf >>

<< Singapore Orchid

STEAMING THE FLOWERS

Due to their fragility, I recommend steaming the orchids and the buds separately before taping them together into a spray. Steam each flower and bud for about 3 seconds to set the colour and to give them a satin-like sheen. Leave to dry for a few minutes.

TAPING THE FLOWERS

Individually tape the wire of each orchid and bud with nile green florist tape (step 15).

Take the white 20-gauge wire, hold a bud about 1cm above this wire and tape them together using the green florist tape.

Continue taping down the wire, adding a bud every 2.5cm along to reveal 1–2cm of the stem, and add an orchid every 5cm (step 16), placing them alternately on the left and the right sides of the stem.

Once you have added the last orchid, finish taping to the end of the wire and trim off the tip with wire scissors.

TO DECORATE THE CAKE

Push the end of the stem into a plastic flower pick and push it into the middle of the top tier. Adjust the position of the orchids and buds with tweezers, if necessary.

MOTH ORCHID

INGREDIENTS

To make a spray of 8 moth orchids and 6 buds:

About 500g white flower paste

White vegetable fat

Food paste colour in gooseberry and claret (both from Sugarflair)

Petal dust in citrus green, primrose (both from Rainbow) and plum (from Sugarflair)

Edible glue

3 white 24-gauge florist wires, each cut into 3 even pieces

2 white 26-gauge florist wires, each cut into 4 even pieces

1 white 20-gauge wire

Nile green florist tape

Small amount of vodka

1 plastic flower pick

EQUIPMENT

Basic tool kit (see page 11)

Moth orchid cutter set (from Peggy Porschen)

Orchid petal veiner (from SK Great Impressions)

Tweezers

Dresden tool

Bone tool

Frilling cone tool

Celpin

Wire scissors

Very fine artist's paintbrush

Small wide artist's paintbrush

Polystyrene cake dummy

to recreate the cake you will need a 2-tier stacked cake made up of the following: 1 round cake measuring 10cm in diameter and 10cm high (top tier); a 15cm-square cake measuring 10cm high (bottom tier). Both cakes are covered with marzipan and pale green sugar paste and are trimmed around the bases with 15mm-wide lime green satin ribbon. The bottom tier sits on a 23cm-square cake drum covered with pale green sugar paste and trimmed around the edges with 15mm-wide lime green satin ribbon.

Each orchid is made up of 1 wired throat with a pod in the middle, a sepal and 2 petals (using a double petal cutter).

Knead the white flower paste until smooth and pliable. If it feels firm and sticky, add a small dab of white vegetable fat. Wrap the paste in a plastic bag to prevent it from drying out.

MAKING THE MOTH ORCHIDS

Bend one end of each 24-gauge wire into an open hook.

To make the orchid throat, roll out some flower paste on the plastic board, over the largest Mexican hat.

Flip the paste over, place the moth orchid throat cutter with the 2 side petals centred over the Mexican hat, then cut out the throat shape (step 1).

Place the throat shape on the foam pad with the Mexican hat sitting in a hole (step 2), then thin the edges with a bone tool (step 3).

Hold the throat shape between your fingers and push a small well into the middle of the Mexican hat using the frilling cone tool.

Brush a small amount of edible glue inside the well and push one of the 24-gauge wires through the middle (step 4) until the hook anchors in the Mexican hat.

Pinch the Mexican hat paste along the wire at the back of the throat, to create a long neck.

Curl up the long pointed ends of the throat and the side petals using a Celpin (step 5).

Push the wire through the well of a perforated foam mat so the throat sits in a dip (step 6). Place the mat over a bowl or plastic container to allow room for the wire underneath and leave the throat to dry overnight.

Repeat this process to make the remaining 7 orchid throats.

To make the little pods, shape 8 balls, measuring about 4mm in diameter, using the white flower paste.

Shape them into ovals and run the thin end of a Dresden tool lengthways down the middle to make a groove. Leave to dry overnight.

Once dry, brush the pods and the inner petal edges of the throats with primrose petal dust.

Using a very fine artist's paintbrush and plum petal dust, paint lines on the throats, from the middle to the side petals and along the edge of the upper petal.

Brush the middle of each throat with edible glue and stick the little pod inside (step 7). Leave to dry on a polystyrene cake dummy.

To make the sepals (the 3 narrow petals) and orchid petals, roll out more flower paste, with the paste for the sepal over a large Mexican hat.

Centre the 3-petal cutter (for the sepals) over the Mexican hat and the double petal cutter (for the petals) over a smooth section of paste and cut out the shapes.

Ball the edges of the sepal and petals using a Celpin (see page 219).

Press each petal in the orchid petal veiner (step 8).

Brush the sepal centre with edible glue and centre the orchid petals on top, with 1 sepal petal in the middle.

To join the 2 parts of the flower together, push the petal centre down with the end of a paintbrush (step 9), then leave it to set in the well of a perforated foam mat (step 10) for about 15 minutes, until the flower paste feels leathery.

Repeat the process for the remaining 7 orchids.

Dilute a small amount of claret food paste colour with a drop of vodka to make a liquid paint. Flick the paint over the throats using a small wide artist's paintbrush (step 11). Leave the throats to dry.

Brush a thin layer of glue in the petal centre and stick the throat in the middle (step 12).

Press the paste of the Mexican hat along the wire to create a long neck, then place the orchid in the well of a perforated foam mat. To allow room for the wire underneath, rest the mat over a bowl or plastic container.

Repeat for the remaining orchids and leave to dry overnight.

Continued overleaf >>

MAKING THE BUDS

Mix the remaining flower paste with gooseberry food paste colour and make 6 balls measuring about 6mm in diameter, then shape them into ovals.

Dip the end of a 26-gauge wire in edible glue and push it halfway into the bud lengthways.

Using a kitchen knife, score the sides of the bud to make 4 equal sections. Pinch the top of the bud into a small tip using tweezers.

Repeat to make the remaining buds and leave to dry overnight. (See steps 12–14, page 142.)

Once dry, brush the buds all over with citrus green petal dust.

STEAMING THE FLOWERS

Due to their fragility, I recommend steaming the orchids and the buds separately before taping them together into a spray. Steam each flower and bud for about 3 seconds to set the colours and give them a satin-like sheen. Leave to dry for a few minutes.

TAPING THE FLOWERS

Individually tape the wire of each orchid and bud with nile green florist tape.

Take the white 20-gauge wire, hold a bud about 1cm above this wire and tape them together using the green florist tape.

Continue taping down the wire, adding a bud every 2.5cm along to reveal about 2cm of the stem, and add an orchid every 5cm, placing them alternately on the left and right sides of the stem. After every few orchids, add a couple of buds.

After adding the last orchid, finish taping to the end of the wire and trim off the tip with wire scissors.

TO DECORATE THE CAKE

Push the end of the stem into a plastic flower pick and push it into the middle of the top tier. Adjust the position of the orchids and buds with tweezers, if necessary.

WHITE CATTLEYA ORCHID

INGREDIENTS

To make a bouquet of 6 cattleya orchids:
About 400g white flower paste
White vegetable fat
Petal dust in primrose (one each from Sugarflair and Rainbow)
Edible glue
3 white 24-gauge florist wires, each cut in half
6 white 26-gauge wires, each cut into 5 equal lengths
White florist tape
1 plastic flower pick
Cornflour in a muslin pouch, for dusting

EQUIPMENT

Basic tool kit (see page 11)
Cattleya orchid cutter set (from Peggy Porschen)
Leaf veining mat (from FMM, part of the veining mats 1–4 set)
Veining board
Bone tool
Dresden tool
Celstick
Tweezers
Wire scissors
Perforated foam mat
Polystyrene cake dummy

METHOD

to recreate the cake you will need a round cake, measuring 10cm in diameter and 10cm high, covered with marzipan and pale green sugar paste and trimmed around the sides with 15mm-wide lime green satin ribbon. The cake sits on a round 15cm-diameter cake card covered with pale green sugar paste.

Each cattleya orchid consists of a wired column with a lip petal attached, 2 wired frilly petals and 3 wired pointed petals, also called sepals.

Knead the white flower paste until smooth and pliable. If it feels firm and sticky add a dab of white vegetable fat. Wrap it in a plastic bag until ready to use to prevent it drying out.

MAKING THE COLUMN
You will need 6 white flower paste balls measuring about 7mm in diameter.

Shape each ball into a cone, dip the end of a 24-gauge wire in glue and push it a third of the way into the cone from the tip. Repeat for the remaining 5 balls.

Place one cone at a time on the foam pad and hollow it out with a small bone tool (step 1).

Pinch the base slightly and pinch a tip in the top of the column using tweezers (step 2). Follow the tip around the back of the column and pinch the paste along the centre to make a line.

Repeat for the remaining columns and leave to dry overnight.

MAKING THE THROAT AND LIP
Roll out some white flower paste to a thickness of about 1mm. Cut out a throat and lip shape using the fluted petal cutter.

Place the shape on a foam pad, score down the centre with the thin end of a Dresden tool (step 3) and ball the edges with a Celpin (step 4).

Transfer the paste to a plastic board lightly dusted with cornflour, then frill the fluted edges using a Celstick (step 5).

Brush the straight edges of the throat with edible glue and fold them over the back of the cone (step 6). The edges should meet and overlap slightly towards the column base.

Bend the frilled lip downwards to open it up and create air between the lip and the column. Push the wire into a polystyrene cake dummy and leave to dry overnight.

Repeat for the remaining orchid throats.

MAKING THE FRILLY PETALS
Roll out some white flower paste on a veining board, to a thickness of about 1mm.

Turn the paste over and cut out a petal using the wider petal cutter, with the vein running from 1 tip to the other (step 7).

Place the petal on a foam pad, dip the end of a 26-gauge wire in edible glue and insert it about halfway into the thicker end of the vein.

Turn the petal over and press the leaf veining mat on top to emboss it with lines (step 8).

Lightly dust a plastic board with cornflour, lay the petal on the board – embossed side down – and frill the edges using a Celstick (step 9).

Pinch the base of the petal along the wire.

Hold the wire down with your finger, near the bottom of the petal and bend the exposed wire up (step 10).

Place the petal over a raised area on the perforated mat and let it dry overnight (step 11).

Repeat to make another 11 frilly petals.

MAKING THE PLAIN-EDGED PETALS
Repeat the process as for the frilly petals but using the narrower petal cutter.

After embossing with the leaf veining mat, turn the petal over and score a line along the middle using the thin end of the Dresden tool (step 12).

Pinch the base of the petal along the wire, bend the wire as in step 10 and lay the petal over a raised part of the perforated foam mat (step 13). Leave to dry overnight.

Repeat to make another 17 petals.

DUSTING THE FLOWERS
Brush the inside of the orchid throats and the bottom and centre of the petals with a blend of the 2 primrose petal dusts. The colour should fade out towards the outer edges (step 14).

TAPING THE FLOWERS
Hold the throat with the frilly lip at 6 o'clock. Add the 2 frilly petals at the back at 10 and 2 o'clock (step 15). Tape them together using white florist tape.

Add 2 plain-edged petals at 8 and 4 o'clock and the third petal at 12 o'clock (step 16). Tape them in place. Continue to tape along the stem.

STEAMING THE FLOWERS
Steam each orchid for about 3 seconds to set the colours and give them a satin-like sheen.

TO DECORATE THE CAKE
Tape the orchids together to form a bouquet, and, using a flower pick, push the stem into the centre of the cake top.

BLUSH ANEMONES

THIS STUNNING FLOWER IS BASED
ON THE WHITE FRENCH ANEMONE.
I TINTED THE PETALS NUDE
AND POWDER PINK TO CREATE
A CHIC PARISIAN FEEL,
WHILE THE INKY CENTRES GIVE
THE DESIGN A LUXE LOOK.

INGREDIENTS

To make 2 wired anemones:
About 250g white flower paste
White vegetable fat
Food paste colour in black extra, dusky pink (both from Sugarflair) and ivory (from Wilton)
Petal dust in black magic, cream (both from Rainbow) and dusky pink (from Sugarflair)
Edible glue
Bunch of small black round stamen
1 teaspoon fine semolina
6 white 26-gauge florist wires, each cut into quarters
1 white 24-gauge florist wire, cut in half
1 white 22-gauge florist wire, cut in half
White florist tape

EQUIPMENT

Basic tool kit (see page 11)
Small and large anemone petal cutters and silicone anemone petal veiner (a set from Petal Crafts)
Veining board
Tweezers
Bone tool
Wire scissors
Flat artist's paintbrush
Polystyrene cake dummy
Perforated foam mat
2 plastic flower picks

METHOD

to recreate the cake you will need a round Victoria sponge measuring 15cm in diameter and 10cm high, covered with pink buttercream. To achieve the design around the sides of the cake, I used a patterned-edge side scraper for the second masking coat.

Mix the white flower paste with a small amount of vegetable fat and knead it until smooth and pliable.

Mix about 50g of the flower paste with black food paste colour and the remaining flower paste with a little ivory and dusky pink food paste colour to a pale nude shade.

MAKING THE ANEMONE CENTRES
Using the black paste, make 2 ball shapes measuring about 9mm in diameter, or the size of a hazelnut.

Using tweezers, bend one end of each 22-gauge wire into an open hook.

Dip the hooks in edible glue and stick each one halfway into a black ball of flower paste (step 1).

Mix the semolina with a small amount of black magic petal dust and transfer to the well of a paint palette or a small round dish.

Brush the tops of the black paste balls with a thin coating of edible glue and dip them in the semolina, turning to cover completely (step 2).

Push the wire into a polystyrene cake dummy and leave to dry overnight.

Divide the bunch of black stamen in half. Bend 1 end of each 24-gauge wire into a large open hook and wind them around a bunch of stamen.

Push the stamen up, either side of the wire (step 3), and gather them at the top.

Tape them together with the florist tape (step 4) and push the cone of a Celpin into the middle to make a crater.

When the black ball shapes are dry, push one into the middle of each bunch of stamen (step 5) and spread the stamen evenly around the outside.

Tape the wires together with white florist tape, wrapping it tightly underneath the stamen to hold them in place.

MAKING THE ANEMONE PETALS
You will need 6 small and 6 large petals per flower, so 24 petals in total to make 2 flowers.

Roll out some nude flower paste on a veining board, until the paste is very thin. You should almost see the vein showing through.

Flip the paste over and cut out a petal shape with the thicker part of the pencil vein running through the tip of the cutter (step 6).

Place the petal on a foam pad and thin the edges with a Celpin.

Dip the end of a 26-gauge wire in edible glue and push it about one-third of the way into the pencil vein.

Turn the petal over and press the anemone petal veiner on top to emboss (step 7).

Use a bone tool to make the petal edges slightly wavy.

Run the thin end of a Dresden tool from the base to the tip of the petal to make a central vein (step 8).

Pinch along the wire at the base of the petal to remove any excess paste.

Curl back the sides of the petal using a cocktail stick (step 9).

Place the petal in the well of a paint palette and push the wire down into the curve of the well.

Repeat the process for the remaining petals and leave to dry overnight.

DUSTING THE ANEMONES
Using a flat artist's paintbrush, dust the anemone petals with a blend of dusky pink and cream petal dust, working from the base of the petal upwards and from the petal edges downwards (step 10).

STEAMING THE ANEMONES
Steam the petals for a few seconds to set the colour and give them a satin-like sheen.

TAPING THE ANEMONES
Sharply bend each petal wire downwards to an angle of 90°.

Arrange 3 small petals evenly around the anemone centre and tape them to the stem (step 11), then place 3 more small petals in between.

One by one, arrange the 6 large petals underneath and in between the small petals, taping each one in place (step 12). Then tape all the way down the stem and trim the end with scissors.

Repeat for the second flower.

Push each stem into a plastic flower pick, then stick them into the cake.

VINTAGE BLOOMS

THIS FLORAL DESIGN HAS BEEN
THE NUMBER ONE CHOICE
WITH MY BRIDES SINCE THE RISE
OF THE VINTAGE-STYLE WEDDING.
THE BEAUTIFUL COMBINATION
OF BLUSH PINK ROSES AND FADED
GREEN HYDRANGEAS CREATES A SOFT,
ROMANTIC VIBE.

INGREDIENTS

To make 1 open rose, 1 half-open rose, 1 large and 1 small rosebud with leaves,
about 20 hydrangeas and about 20 medium and 20 small stephanotis blossoms:

About 1kg white flower paste

Food paste colour in dusky pink, gooseberry (both from Sugarflair)
and moss green (from Wilton)

Petal dust in dusky pink, aubergine (both from Sugarflair)
and citrus green (from Rainbow)

White vegetable fat

Edible glue

White and nile green florist tape

Small amount of royal icing, soft-peak consistency (see pages 216–17)

2 large, 1 medium and 1 small polystyrene buds (I used ones from Celbud)

4 white 22-gauge wires (roses)

3 white 26-gauge wires, each cut into thirds (leaves)

14 white 26-gauge florist wires, each cut into thirds (stephanotis)

7 white 26-gauge florist wires, each cut into thirds (hydrangeas)

EQUIPMENT

Basic tool kit (see page 11)

Small, medium and large rose petal cutters (from Peggy Porschen)

Medium and large rose calyx cutters (from Peggy Porschen)

Large and medium rose leaf cutters

Rose leaf veiner (from Diamond Paste)

Small and medium stephanotis cutters

Hydrangea petal cutter

Hydrangea petal veiner

Fine craft scissors

Tweezers

Bone tool

Dresden tool

Flat wide artist's paintbrush

Silicone tray with 6cm half-sphere moulds

Polystyrene cake dummy

Large paper cupcake case

Paper piping bag

METHOD

to recreate the cake you will need a round cake measuring 15cm in diameter and 15cm high, covered with marzipan and white sugar paste. The base of the cake is trimmed with 2 satin ribbons: 25mm wide in pale pink; 15mm wide in mauve. Tiny white dots are piped around the sides of the cake with soft-peak royal icing.

MAKING THE ROSES AND BUDS

Create a tunnel through the base of each polystyrene bud using a cocktail stick.

Thread a 22-gauge wire through each polystyrene bud, position the bud in the middle of the wire and bend the wire around the base.

Twist the wires together to make a stem and ensure that there is no gap between the bud and the wire.

Mix about 400g of white flower paste with dusky pink food paste colour and roll it out to a thickness of about 1mm.

Check which size of cutter fits each polystyrene bud; the bud should fit just inside the petal cutter. I use the small cutter for the smallest and medium buds, and the medium cutter for the large buds. Cut out a petal for each one.

Place a petal on a foam pad and ball it with the Celpin (see page 219). The petal edges should become slightly wavy.

Turn the petal over and brush it with a thin layer of edible glue.

Lay the petal over the polystyrene bud, rounded side up. The tip of the bud should sit centred about 5mm below the petal edge.

Fold the left edge of the petal over the tip of the bud, pinch it together at the top, then fold the right edge.

The tip of the polystyrene bud should be completely enclosed, with only the right-hand edge of the petal left slightly open (step 1).

Leave the smallest bud as it is. Make 3 more petals for each of the other roses, using the same cutter as before for each one. This time, only brush the bottom part of each petal with glue, in a 'V' shape; brush the glue two-thirds up the left edge and halfway up the right edge.

Before attaching the first petal of the second layer, brush the polystyrene bud with glue, just below the join of the first petal (step 2).

Lay the bud on the next petal, with the join centred underneath. The tip should sit about 5mm below the petal edge (step 3).

Fold down the left edge of the petal and leave the right side open.

Turn the rosebud clockwise and stick the second petal halfway over the previous one, folding down the left side and leaving the right side open.

Add the third petal halfway over the previous one and tuck it under the second petal (step 4).

Make sure that the 3 petals in this layer are spaced out evenly and that they all sit at the same height (step 5).

Using a cocktail stick, fold back the open side on the right of each petal (step 6). The best way to do this is to hold the petal edge with your finger as you wrap and pull the paste around the stick. The cocktail stick should be kept parallel to the tip of the bud to maintain

the cone shape; otherwise the rose will open up too much.

Once you have folded back all the petals from the right, repeat on the left. Take care not to poke the cocktail stick through the paste.

Gently pinch each petal at the top to create a soft tip.

Leave the medium polystyrene bud as it is. Make 5 more petals for each of the remaining 2 roses using the same cutter as before.

Once you have balled the petals (step 7), fold back the sides and the top edge with a cocktail stick. Gently pinch the corners (step 8).

Again, brush the base of each petal with glue in a 'V' shape (step 9), then stick the first petal onto the bud, laying it over a join, this time positioning the petal at the same height as the previous layer (step 10).

Arrange the remaining 4 petals in the same way as before – over the petal on the left and under the petal on the right.

Leave the petals to dry, ideally overnight.

For the large open rose, roll out some more paste for the next layer. Cut out 7 petals using the largest rose petal cutter.

Ball the petals as before, then fold back the edges and pinch the corners, as in step 8.

Place them in a paint palette with the folded edges overhanging and the tips sitting curved inside the well to create a cup shape. Let the petals start to set, until they feel leathery.

Meanwhile, make 9 petals for the final layer. Lay the petals in the half-sphere moulds with the edges curled over the sides. They should be more open than the petals in the previous layer.

Once the 7 petals have set, take them out of the paint palette and brush a 'V' shape of edible glue onto the base of each one.

Arrange the first petal over a join as before, placing it slightly lower than the previous layer of petals (step 11).

Turn the rose over and attach the remaining 6 petals from the back, as this will make it easier to handle them (step 12). Interlock the petals in the same way as before.

Check that the rose looks even from the top, adjusting the petals if necessary, and let the rose dry upside down on a soft surface, such as a polystyrene cake dummy, for 30 minutes.

Apply the final layer of 9 petals in the same way as the previous layer, arranging them as low as possible – the base of each petal should touch the wire.

Leave the rose to dry upside down for about 15 minutes, then turn it over and place it in a paper cupcake case to dry completely. This will allow the petals to open up a little, without falling off the rose centre (step 13).

MAKING THE CALYXES

To make the calyxes, mix about 150g of white flower paste with moss green food paste colour and roll it out to a thickness of about 1mm.

Cut out 2 medium calyxes for the rosebuds and 2 large calyxes for the half-open and open rose. Make a few snips into the edges of each calyx petal using fine craft scissors (step 14).

Widen and thin out the calyx petals with a bone tool (step 15).

Flip the calyxes over and brush thinly with edible glue. Take a medium calyx and push the wire of a rosebud through the middle (step 16).

Bend the calyx petals upwards and stick them to the sides of the rosebud. Ensure that any untidy areas beneath the rosebud are completely covered.

Repeat for the remaining roses and buds using the appropriate calyx size.

MAKING THE ROSE LEAVES

You will need 3 sets of leaves, each made up of 1 large and 2 medium leaves.

Roll out the remaining green flower paste on a veining board.

Centre a leaf cutter with the bottom over the thicker end of the vein.

Cut out 3 large and 6 medium leaves.

Place one of the leaves on a foam mat, vein facing upwards.

Push a 26-gauge wire dipped in glue about one-third of the way into the base of the vein (step 17). Press the leaf in a rose leaf veiner, with the raised pattern on the top (step 18).

Place the leaf on a perforated foam mat to dry (step 19).

Repeat for the remaining leaves and allow them to dry overnight.

DUSTING THE ROSES

Dust the petal edges of the roses and buds with dusky pink petal dust, using a flat wide artist's paintbrush (step 20).

Dust the leaves with citrus green dust, working from the base upwards and from the sides to the centre (step 21). Mix a little aubergine petal dust into the green dust and brush it over the leaf edges.

Lightly brush the calyxes with citrus green dust; take care not to stain the pink petals (step 22).

TAPING THE FLOWER TOGETHER

Take the large leaves and wind nile green florist tape around the top of the wire, covering about 1 cm (step 23).

Sharply bend the wires of the smaller leaves sideways to an angle of 90° – 3 leaves should point to the right and 3 to the left.

Take a large leaf and position 2 small leaves on either side at exactly the same height. Tape them into position by winding green florist tape around all 3 wires (step 24).

Wind the tape a few centimetres along the wire, then pull the wires of the smaller leaves down so that the upper parts of the wires disappear underneath the tape (step 25).

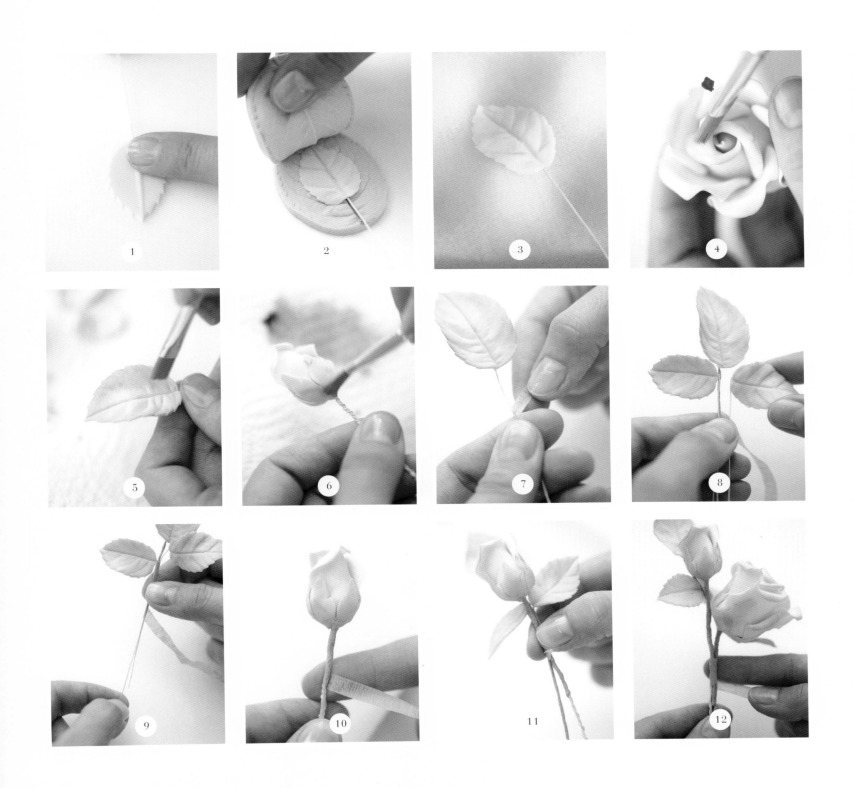

Repeat to complete all 3 sets of leaves.

Tape the stems of the roses and rosebuds (step 26), then tape a bud, 2 sets of leaves and the half-open rose together to make a spray (steps 27–8). Tape the remaining set of leaves to the stem of the large rose.

MAKING THE STEPHANOTIS
Using tweezers, bend one end of each 26-gauge wire into a small open hook.

Knead about 150g of white flower paste until smooth and pliable.

Roll out a strip of paste over a medium Mexican hat, to a thickness of 1mm. Centre the stephanotis cutter over the Mexican hat and cut out a blossom (step 29).

Place the blossom – Mexican hat upwards – on a foam pad and use the wider end of a Dresden tool to curl the petals upwards.

Dip the hook into edible glue and push the wire through the centre until the hook anchors inside the Mexican hat (step 30).

Pinch the paste of the Mexican hat along the wire to create a long neck.

Place the blossom upside down on a foam pad and reshape the petals by running a bone tool from the edge to the middle (step 31). Repeat to make about 20 medium and 20 small blossoms and let dry overnight.

Put the royal icing in a piping bag and pipe a small dot into the middle of the stephanotis flowers (step 32).

Tape the stephanotis together in bunches of 3 (using blossoms of the same size for each), using white florist tape.

MAKING THE HYDRANGEAS
Mix about 150g of white flower paste with gooseberry food paste colour. If the paste feels a little too firm and sticky, add a dab of white vegetable fat. Wrap the paste in a plastic bag until ready to use to prevent it from drying out.

To make the hydrangea centres, roll a small amount of paste into a thin sausage. Divide it into 20 ball shapes, about 3mm in diameter.

Form each ball into a teardrop shape. Dip the end of a white 26-gauge wire in edible glue and push it into the tip of one of the teardrops (step 33).

Shape the upper part of the teardrop into a ball and flatten it.

Score the top with a kitchen knife (step 34) to make 4 equal sections. Push the wire into a polystyrene cake dummy and leave to dry overnight.

Once the hydrangea centres are dry, roll out a thin piece of green flower paste over a large Mexican hat.

Centre the hydrangea cutter over the Mexican hat and cut out the blossom (step 35).

Press the blossom in the hydrangea petal veiner, taking care not to flatten the Mexican hat too much (step 36).

Brush the centre of the blossom with edible glue and push the wire of a hydrangea centre into the Mexican hat (step 37).

Push the blossom against the centre and let it dry upside down over the dip of a perforated foam mat (step 38). Repeat for the remaining hydrangea blossoms.

Once dry, dust the petal edges with a blend of dusky pink, aubergine and citrus green petal dust (step 39).

Tape together clusters of 3 hydrangeas using white florist tape (step 40).

STEAMING THE FLOWERS
Steam the roses, rose leaves and hydrangea blossoms for about 3 seconds to set the colours and give them a satin-like sheen.

TO DECORATE THE CAKE
You can either tape all flowers together to make a bouquet, then push it into the centre of the cake top using tweezers, or you can stick the flowers into the cake individually. Put the wires into plastic flower picks before inserting them into the cake.

Use tweezers to bend the flowers and blossoms into shape once they are in place on the cake.

CHERRY BLOSSOMS

THIS DESIGN SHOWCASES SPRING'S MOST PRIZED FLOWER, WITH ENOUGH SUGAR CHERRY BLOSSOMS TO ADORN EVERY SLICE WHEN THE CAKE IS SERVED.

INGREDIENTS

To make one spray of about 5 large, 5 medium and
5 small cherry blossoms, 5 buds and 5 leaves:

About 150g white flower paste

White vegetable fat

Food paste colour in claret and gooseberry (from Sugarflair)

Petal dust in plum (from Sugarflair) and citrus green (from Rainbow)

Edible glue

White small round stamen (you will need less than a bunch)

7 x 28-gauge florist wires, each cut into quarters

White 20-gauge florist wire

Brown florist tape

EQUIPMENT

Basic tool kit (see page 11)

Cherry blossom cutter set of 3 (from Peggy Porschen)

Cherry blossom veiner (from Sunflower Sugar Art)

Multipurpose leaf cutter, 15mm x 35mm (from Peggy Porschen)

Miniature leaf veiner (from Diamond Paste)

Tweezers

Plastic flower pick

CHERRY 172 BLOSSOMS

METHOD

to recreate the cake you will need a stacked 2-tier round cake measuring 10cm in diameter and 10cm high (top tier), and 15cm in diameter and 10cm high (bottom tier). All tiers are covered with marzipan and ivory sugar paste. The bottom tier sits on a 23cm-diameter round cake drum covered with ivory sugar paste and trimmed around the edge with 15mm-wide ivory pearl satin ribbon.

To make the cake shown on page 171, you will need 3 round cake layers measuring 15cm in diameter, made using the rich dark chocolate cake recipe (see page 201). The layers are sandwiched together and topped with vanilla buttercream (see page 203) coloured pink.

Each spray of cherry blossoms is made up of a mixture of large, medium and small blossoms, as well as little buds and leaves. You can combine them and make up the sprays to suit your cake; however, I would always recommend using an uneven number of blossoms: perhaps 3 or 5 of each size and type. It is also useful to have extra individual blossoms and small clusters to fill in any gaps or to sprinkle over your cake. Use the following method as a starting point and scale the number of cherry blossom sprays up or down according to your requirements. As a guide, I used 6 sprays for my 2-tier cake.

Mix 100g of white flower paste with a tiny amount of claret food paste colour to make a very pale pink shade, and mix the remaining 50g of flower paste with gooseberry food colour to make a pale green. Wrap the pastes in plastic bags and leave to rest for 15 minutes.

MAKING THE CENTRES
Bend the end of a 28-gauge wire into a small open hook, using tweezers.

Take 3 stamen, gather them in the middle and tuck them underneath the hook, then bend them up (step 1).

Close the hook firmly to hold the stamen in place.

Repeat to make another 14 sets of wired stamen.

Wrap tape over each wire hook and the bottom of the stamen using brown florist tape (step 2).

Brush the stamen generously with plum petal dust until they are cerise pink (step 3).

MAKING THE CHERRY BLOSSOMS
Roll out a strip of pink paste over a suitably sized hole for a Mexican hat to a thickness of about 1mm.

Flip the paste over and centre the cherry blossom cutter over the Mexican hat. Cut out the blossom (step 4).

Place the blossom, Mexican hat facing down, inside the bottom half of a cherry blossom veiner. Ensure the blossom is centred with the petals aligned with the shape of the veiner (step 5).

Place the upper part of the cherry blossom veiner on top and press gently around the edges, with minimal pressure in the middle to avoid flattening the Mexican hat. If the paste sticks to the veiner, rub the veiner with a thin layer of vegetable fat.

Remove the blossom from the veiner and leave to set for a few minutes.

Take the wired stamen and brush the upper part of the brown tape with edible glue, just underneath the stamen.

Push the wire all the way into the middle of the blossom (step 6) until the tape has disappeared and only the stamen are showing.

Pinch the paste of the Mexican hat up the wire to create a long neck at the back of the cherry blossom. Ensure a clean finish where the paste meets the tape.

Lay the blossom on a perforated foam mat and leave to dry overnight. Repeat for the remaining cherry blossoms.

MAKING THE BUDS
Using the remaining pink flower paste, roll 5 ball shapes each measuring about 2mm in diameter.

Dip the end of a 28-gauge wire in edible glue and stick it halfway into one of the paste balls.

Shape the ball into an oval bud.

Using a kitchen knife, score the bud to make 4 equal-sized sections (step 7).

Repeat the process to make another 4 buds and leave to dry overnight.

MAKING THE LEAVES
Roll out the green flower paste on a veining board to a thickness of about 1mm.

Flip the paste over and centre the multipurpose leaf cutter lengthways over the vein. Cut out the shape.

Dip the end of a 28-gauge wire in edible glue and push it about halfway into the wider end of the vein.

Emboss the leaf with veins using the most fitting shape of mini leaf veiner (step 8). I cut my mini leaf veiner in half as I found it easier to work with.

Place the leaf on a perforated foam mat, on a curve, and leave to dry overnight (step 9).

Repeat to make a total of 5 leaves.

DUSTING THE FLOWERS

Brush the cherry blossom centres and the tips of the buds with plum petal dust, and the leaves and the base of the buds with citrus green (step 10).

TAPING THE FLOWERS

Take some of the buds and leaves and tape the wires from the top to about halfway down, using the brown florist tape.

Tape together individual clusters of 2 or 3 large and medium blossoms with a leaf, or 2 blossoms with a bud.

Tape 1 bud to the top of a 20-gauge wire using a long thin strip of brown florist tape.

Add an untaped leaf about 5mm below the bud (step 11), followed by an untaped bud, and tape them to the main wire.

Wind tape a few centimetres along the wire, pull down the exposed wires of the leaf and bud until they sit tightly against the stem and the exposed wires disappear inside the tape.

Continue taping down the stem, adding a cluster of blossoms, leaves and buds every few centimetres (step 12). The blossoms should gradually increase in size and fullness as you work towards the bottom of the stem. Every now and then, add an untaped bud or leaf in between the clusters, positioned close to the stem.

Once you have added all the blossoms, continue taping down the wire as far as possible. Only trim the end once you know how much stem you need to drape over the edge of the cake.

STEAMING THE CHERRY BLOSSOMS

Steam each cherry blossom spray for about 3 seconds to set the colours and give them a satin-like sheen.

TO DECORATE THE CAKE

Trim the end of the cherry blossom stem to the required length and push it into a plastic flower pick before sticking it into the cake. Bend the stem to create a sweeping curve and twist out the little blossoms, leaves and buds using tweezers.

CAMELLIA LACE

WITH ITS DELICATE SOFT, ROUNDED
PETALS AND GENTLE CURVES,
THE CAMELLIA IS A CHIC
AND UNDERSTATED FLOWER THAT
MAKES A PERFECT DECORATION
FOR AN ELEGANT CONTEMPORARY CAKE.

INGREDIENTS

To make 1 camellia:

About 200g white flower paste

White vegetable fat

Edible glue

Polystyrene ball, 4cm in diameter

Cornflour in a muslin pouch, for dusting

EQUIPMENT

Basic tool kit (see page 11)

Round pastry cutter, 8cm in diameter

Camellia petal cutter (from Peggy Porschen)

Poppy petal veiner (from Diamond Paste)

3 silicone trays with 6cm half-sphere moulds

Mug with clingfilm stretched over the top

Kitchen paper

TO DECORATE THE CAKE

About 500g royal icing

'Camellia Rose' stencil (from Designer Stencils)

Side scraper

Non-slip turntable

Metal pins (optional)

METHOD

to recreate the cake you will need a stacked 3-tier round cake, measuring 10cm (top tier), 15cm (middle tier) and 20cm (bottom tier) in diameter. All 3 tiers are 12cm high and are covered with marzipan and blush pink sugar paste. The bottom tier sits on a 30cm-diameter round cake drum covered with blush pink sugar paste and trimmed around the edge with 15mm-wide bridal white satin ribbon.

Push a cocktail stick halfway into the polystyrene ball.

Roll out the flower paste to a thickness of about 1mm and cut out a round shape using the round pastry cutter.

Brush the polystyrene ball with edible glue and cover it with the flower paste disc.

Smooth the paste down the sides of the ball with your hand (step 1) and let it set.

Start with the petals for the outer layers of the camellia – these have to set before they can be used. Cut out several petal shapes using the camellia petal cutter (step 2).

Place the petals on a foam pad and ball the edges using a Celpin (see page 219).

Press each camellia petal in the petal veiner (step 3).

Hold the petal in a cupped hand and pinch the top edge slightly.

Place the petal in the well of a sphere mould dusted with cornflour and leave to dry until it feels leathery.

Repeat to make a total of 17 petals.

For the first layer make 3 more petals, repeating the techniques used to make the outer petals.

Brush the surface of each petal, except for the top, with edible glue and stick them over the flower centre, evenly interlocking them. An area the size of a penny should be visible at the top (steps 4–5). The petal bases should touch the cocktail stick at the back of the flower.

Once the petals in the sphere moulds are slightly set, take 5 of the petals and brush the bottom edges with a 'V' shape of edible glue and arrange them evenly around the bud, interlocking them (step 6). Each one should sit over the overlap of 2 petals in the previous layer and open up slightly to reveal the flower centre.

Rest the flower upside down on a soft surface and leave to set for about 30 minutes.

Arrange another 5 petals around the flower in the same way, opening them up more, and, this time, space them out more randomly as they shouldn't all interlock.

Place the camellia upside down on a soft surface and leave to set.

Once set, arrange the last 7 petals in the same random way, until the flower has a full round shape (step 7). You may find it easiest to do this while holding the flower upside down, as the petals can't fall down easily.

Dust the clingfilm-covered mug with cornflour and place the flower on top (step 8). Support the petals with rolled-up strips of kitchen paper to prevent them from closing or opening up too much. Leave to dry completely overnight.

TO DECORATE THE CAKE
Mix the royal icing with enough water to make a smooth soft-peak consistency.

Attach the camellia stencil to the side of the cake (step 9), holding it in place with a pin if necessary.

Place the cake on a turntable. Cover the edge of the side scraper with royal icing (step 10) and scrape it over the stencil, rotating the turntable the opposite way to the direction you are working in (step 11).

Ensure that all the gaps in the stencil are evenly covered, then carefully remove the stencil (step 12).

Let the design dry before continuing on a different part of the same tier. Meanwhile, apply the stencil design to the other tiers.

Once the cake is completely covered with the camellia design and the flower has set, stick the camellia onto the side of the cake with a dab of royal icing.

FLORAL CASCADE

THIS CAKE IS IN FULL BLOOM.
NATURAL BURSTS OF COLOUR
ARE ARTFULLY COMBINED, AS CORAL
CHARM PEONIES, FRENCH LILACS,
PARROT TULIPS AND FREESIAS
CASCADE ELEGANTLY DOWN
A SIMPLE ICED CAKE.

INGREDIENTS

To make about 4 French lilacs, 8 freesias, 5 parrot tulips, 6 open peonies and 6 leaves:

About 2.4kg white flower paste   White vegetable fat

Food paste colour in royal blue, rose, lemon yellow, violet, moss (all from Wilton), gooseberry and claret (both from Sugarflair)

Petal dust in salmon, pale terracotta, cream, strawberry, poppy red, primrose, peach, mauve, spring green,

holly green (all from Rainbow), deep magenta, pink, fuchsia and aubergine (from Sugarflair)

Edible glue   White and nile green florist tape

About 25 flower picks

About 2 bunches tiny round white stamen (for the French lilacs)

8 green 28-gauge florist wires, each cut into quarters (for the French lilacs)

Tiny pointed white stamen, less than a bunch (for the Freesias)

16 white 26-gauge florist wires, each cut into quarters (for the Freesias)

White 22-gauge florist wire (for the Freesias)

5 white 28-gauge florist wires, each cut into 6 (for the Parrot tulip stamen)

3 white 22-gauge florist wires, each cut in half (for the Parrot tulip centres)

10 white 24-gauge florist wires, each cut into thirds (for the Parrot tulip petals)

3 bunches white small pointed stamen (for the Open peonies)

3 white 20-gauge florist wires, each cut in half (for the Open peony centres)

3 white 26-gauge florist wires, halved (for the Open peony stamen)

27 white 26-gauge florist wires, each cut into quarters (for the Open peony petals)

2 white 26-gauge florist wires, each cut into thirds (for the Peony leaves)

EQUIPMENT

Basic tool kit (page 11)

Small and medium lilac blossom cutters (from Peggy Porschen)

Freesia petal cutter (from Peggy Porschen)

Parrot tulip cutter and silicone tulip petal veiner (both from Petal Crafts)

Peony cutter set of 3 (from Peggy Porschen)   Silicone peony petal veining mat (I used one from a Petal Crafts set)

Peony leaf cutter and silicone veiner (both from Sunflower Sugar Art)

Dresden tool or veining tool   Bone tool   Star tool   Frilling cone tool   Celstick

Kitchen knife   Tweezers   Wire scissors   Flat artist's paintbrush

Foam pad with Mexican hat holes   Perforated foam mat   Polystyrene cake dummy

Silicone tray with 6cm half-sphere moulds   Small chocolate egg tray with moulds measuring 6 x 4cm

to recreate the cake you will need a stacked 4-tier round cake, measuring 10cm (top tier), 15cm (second tier), 20cm (third tier) and 25cm (bottom tier) in diameter. All 4 tiers are 12cm high and are covered with marzipan and white sugar paste. The bottom tier sits on a 40cm-diameter round cake drum covered with white sugar paste and trimmed around the edge with 15mm-wide bridal white satin ribbon.

French lilacs

Mix about 400g of white flower paste with a dab of white vegetable fat and knead until smooth and pliable.

Add a small amount of violet food colour and mix the paste to make a lilac shade.

Add a tiny amount of claret food paste colour to about 100g of the lilac paste and mix to make a mauve shade. Wrap the paste in a plastic bag or clingfilm to prevent it from drying out.

MAKING THE BLOSSOMS

Cut off one end of each stamen, leaving the stem as long as possible. You will need about 24 stamen per flower, so 96 in total.

Roll out some of the lilac paste into a thick strip and place it on your plastic board, over the largest Mexican hat hole that will fit the lilac blossom cutter.

Roll out the paste more thinly, then cut out 1 blossom with a Mexican hat and 1 without, using the same-size cutter for both (step 1).

Place both blossoms on a foam pad, with the Mexican hat sitting in the hole (step 2).

Run the wide end of a Dresden tool along each petal from the edge to the centre, to make them wider and curled up (step 3).

Use your fingers to pinch the petal tips (step 4).

Brush a tiny dab of edible glue into the middle of the blossom with the Mexican hat (this should be facing downwards), and place the other blossom on top with the petals in between those of the previous layer.

Push the centre downwards with a star tool, so the petals curl upwards (step 5).

Brush a small amount of edible glue into the centre and push a stamen into the middle.

Press the Mexican hat around the stem of the stamen and twist the paste into a trumpet shape (step 6). Reshape petals with your fingers, if required (step 7).

Repeat this process for the remaining blossoms. You will need about 8 small and 8 medium lilac blossoms per flower. Leave to dry overnight.

MAKING THE BUDS

You will need about 8 buds per flower; 32 in total. Roll the mauve flower paste into a thin sausage, about 5mm thick. Cut it into a combination of small and large (roughly pea-sized) pieces, at a ratio of about two-thirds small to one-third large; you should end up with 32 pieces.

Roll each piece into a ball, then shape it into a teardrop with your fingers.

Dip the end of a green 28-gauge wire in edible glue and push it into the tip of a teardrop, about halfway into the bud (step 8).

Using a kitchen knife, score the top of the bud to make 4 equal-sized sections (step 9) and elongate the bud slightly. Repeat for the remaining buds and leave to dry overnight.

TAPING THE FLOWERS

Once dry, tape the stems of the blossoms and buds individually, from the top to about halfway down using nile green florist tape. As the stems are very delicate, cut the tape into thin strips first.

To assemble the lilacs, start with the smallest bud at the top (step 10) and tape layers of buds and blossoms (step 11), gradually increasing in size as you work down. Add more blossoms with each layer so that the flower becomes wider towards the bottom.

Once all the blossoms have been added, tape down the remaining stems, then trim the ends with wire scissors.

DUSTING THE LILACS

Generously apply a combination of pink and mauve petal dust, using more pink for the buds and more mauve for the blossoms (step 12).

STEAMING THE FLOWERS

Steam the flowers for about 3 seconds to set the colour and to give them a satin-like sheen.

Freesias

Mix 500g of white flower paste with a dab of vegetable fat and knead until smooth and pliable. Wrap the paste in a plastic bag and leave to rest for about 15 minutes.

MAKING THE STAMEN

Using tweezers, bend one end of a white 26-gauge wire into an open hook. Tuck 2 stamen under the hook and bend them upwards in the middle (step 1).

Close the hook and tape up the wire with green florist tape, covering the hook to hold the stamen together (step 2). Make another 23 sets of stamen so you have 3 blossoms per spray.

MAKING THE BUDS

You will need 2 white and 3 green buds for each spray, making the buds gradually smaller. Start with the 2 largest white buds. Roll some white paste into 2 ball shapes, one measuring 8mm in diameter and the other slightly smaller. Shape each ball into a long teardrop.

Dip the end of a white 26-gauge wire in glue and push it halfway into the tip of the teardrop. Using a kitchen knife, score the top to make 3 even sections (step 3). Shape the lower part into a long neck, elongating the upper part. Repeat for the remaining buds and leave to dry.

Mix the leftover white paste with royal blue and lemon colour to make a pale green. Make 24 buds as above, gradually making them smaller.

MAKING THE BLOSSOMS

Each blossom has 2 petal layers. For the first layer, roll some white flower paste into a thick strip and place it on the plastic board, over the largest Mexican hat hole for the freesia cutter.

Cut out the freesia blossom and place it over the hole on the foam pad.

Push the end of a Celpin into the middle of each petal, working towards the blossom centre, so the petals take on a cup shape (step 4).

Run the thin end of a Dresden tool along each petal, from the edge to the base, to emboss 3 lines on each one (step 5).

Hold the blossom with the Mexican hat between your fingertips, and push the tip of a frilling cone tool into the middle.

Dab a little glue into the centre of the blossom and push the wired stamen into the middle until the green tape almost disappears (step 6).

Turn over the blossom and press the Mexican hat along the wire to create a long neck. Gently pinch the petal tips into a soft point.

Repeat this process for the remaining blossoms and hang them over the side of a polystyrene cake dummy to dry, ideally overnight. Make 1 open, 1 half-open and 1 closed blossom per spray by bending the paste inwards or outwards slightly while it is half set.

Once the first layer of petals is dry, make the second layer, but when you put the blossom on the foam pad, the Mexican hat should be facing up. Repeat this process up to step 6.

Brush the blossom centre with glue and gently pinch the petal tips. Push the blossom up the wire of a dry blossom and stick it underneath with the petals in the gaps between those of the first layer (step 7). Apply more glue where the petals meet, to hold them in place.

Pinch the Mexican hat along the wire to form as long a neck as possible, then hang the flower upside down over the side of a polystyrene cake dummy and leave to dry overnight (step 8). Repeat for the remaining blossoms.

DUSTING THE FLOWERS

Brush primrose petal dust onto the white buds, blossom centres and necks (step 9). Mix primrose and spring green dust and brush it over the backs of the blossoms and green buds.

MAKING THE CALYXES

Mix any leftover green paste or about 50g of white flower paste with moss and gooseberry food paste colour to make a dark green. For each bud and blossom make a small ball measuring about 3mm in diameter.

Brush the back of a bud or blossom with edible glue and push the ball up the wire so it sits just underneath the neck. Push the paste up around the neck, turning the stem between your fingers (step 10). Repeat for the remaining buds and blossoms (step 11) and leave to dry.

TAPING THE FLOWERS

Wind green florist tape around the end of a white 22-gauge wire. Hold the smallest green bud close to the wire, about 5mm down from the tip. Wind the tape around the wire of the bud and along the main stem for another 5mm.

Pull the exposed wire of the bud until it disappears and the calyx is against the tape. Add the next smallest bud and continue in the same way, spacing out the buds and blossoms more as they get bigger. Make sure all the buds and blossoms face the same way and are underneath rather than next to each other (step 12).

Bend the end of the flower stem downwards and adjust the buds and blossoms as needed.

STEAMING THE FLOWERS:

Steam the flowers for about 3 seconds to set the colour and to give them a satin-like sheen.

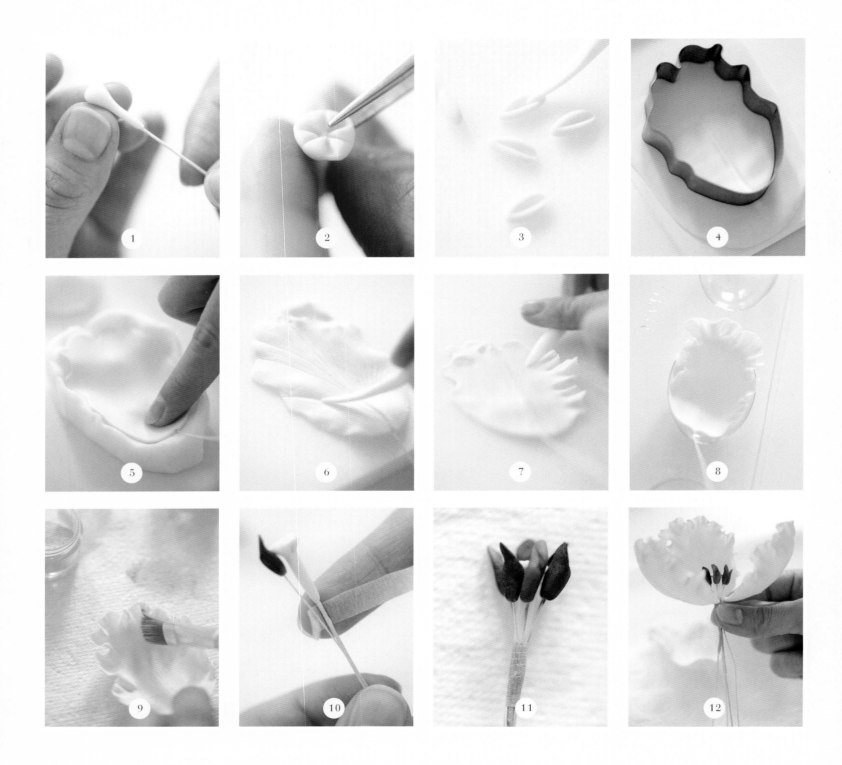

Parrot tulips

Each tulip is made up of 1 tulip centre, 6 stamen and 3 closed and 3 open petals. You will need about 500g of white flower paste.

Mix about 50g with a small amount of gooseberry food paste colour to make a very pale green. Mix the remaining 450g with lemon yellow food colour to make a very pale yellow.

MAKING THE TULIP CENTRES

Roll some of the green paste into 5 ball shapes, about 5mm in diameter. One at a time, place the ball shapes in your hand and roll 1 end into a point to make a long teardrop.

Dip the end of a white 22-gauge wire in edible glue and push it about halfway into the tip of the teardrop.

Twist the paste along the stem until the whole tulip centre is about 2cm long and has a thick round end at the top (step 1).

Flatten the end with your finger and score it into 3 equal sections with a knife.

Using tweezers, pinch the paste in the centre of each section (step 2).

Repeat for the remaining 4 tulip centres and leave to dry overnight.

MAKING THE TULIP STAMEN

Using the green paste, shape another 6 small balls for each tulip, about 3mm in diameter.

Roll each ball into a pod shape, then press the thin end of a Dresden tool along the length of each pod (step 3).

Place the pods on a foam pad, on their side. Flatten the tips using a bone tool.

Dip the 28-gauge wires in edible glue and push each one halfway into the base of a pod. Leave to dry overnight.

MAKING THE TULIP PETALS

Roll out the pale yellow paste on a veining board to a thickness of about 1mm.

Flip over the paste and cut out a tulip petal with the thicker end of the vein running through the centre of the cutter base (step 4).

Place the petal on a foam pad, dip the end of a white 24-gauge wire in edible glue and push it about one-third of the way into the pencil vein.

Turn over the petal and lay it in the base of the tulip petal veiner. Bend the wire into the curve of the petal veiner (step 5).

Press the top of the veiner onto the petal to emboss. Carefully remove the petal from the veiner and place it upside down on a foam pad.

Using the thin end of a Dresden tool, score the petal along the veins, from the petal edges at the top to the bottom centre (step 6).

Flip over the petal and place it on a plastic board lightly dusted with cornflour.

Using a thin Celpin, frill the petal edges (step 7).

Gently pinch along the wire at the bottom of the petal and lay it in the well of a half-sphere mould dusted with cornflour.

Repeat this process for the remaining petals. You will need 6 petals per tulip: 3 petals that have been dried in half-sphere moulds for the inner layer (these will be more closed); and 3 petals that have been dried in chocolate egg trays (step 8) for the outer layer (these will be more open). Leave all the petals to dry overnight.

DUSTING THE FLOWERS

Brush the stamen generously with aubergine petal dust. For the petals, use a mixture of primrose, salmon and pale terracotta petal dust. Brush the front and back of each petal, from the edges to the centres, using a flat artist's paintbrush (step 9). Enhance the veins and edges by dusting them more heavily than the rest of the petal.

TAPING THE FLOWERS

Arrange 6 stamen evenly around each stem, about one-third higher than the tulip centre, and tape them together with green florist tape (steps 10–11).

Sharply bend the petal wires downwards at an angle of 90° at the base of the petal.

One by one, tape 3 closed petals around each stem (step 12); the petal base should sit just underneath the neck of the tulip centre.

Tape 3 open petals around the stem, just underneath and in between the closed petals. Tape all the way down the stem and trim off the end with wire scissors.

STEAMING THE FLOWERS

Bend the stamen and petals outwards slightly. Steam each tulip for about 3 seconds to set the colours and give them a satin-like sheen.

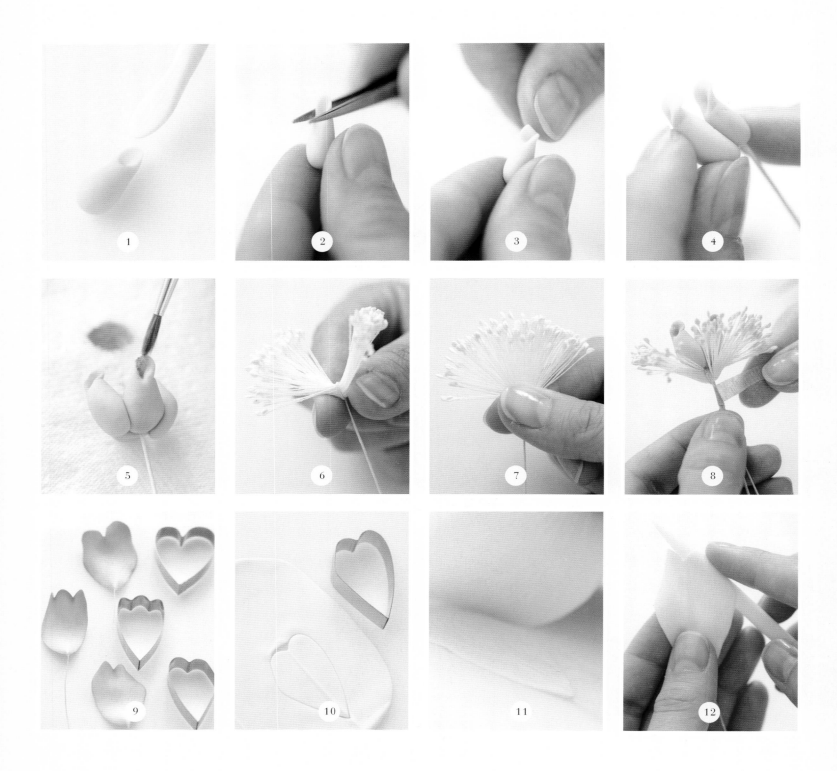

Coral peonies

Each peony is made up of 1 centre, stamen and 3 layers of 6 wired petals.

You will need about 900g of white flower paste. Mix about 200g with gooseberry food paste colour to make a light green shade, and mix the remaining paste with rose food paste colour to make a very pale pink shade. Wrap the pastes in plastic bags and leave to rest for at least 15 minutes.

MAKING THE CENTRES

Each peony centre is made up of 5 individually shaped pods (or buds) with stamen. To make the centre pod, roll some green paste into a ball measuring about 5mm in diameter.

Place the pod in the palm of your hand and shape it into a teardrop.

Lay the teardrop on a foam pad and press down the tip with the wider end of a Dresden tool (step 1).

Using tweezers, pinch the base of the tip and twist and bend it backwards (steps 2–3).

Dip the end of a 20-gauge wire in edible glue and push it halfway into the bottom of the pod. Repeat for the other 5 centre pods and let them dry overnight.

Once dry, make 4 slightly larger pods for each centre, starting with ball shapes about 6mm in diameter. Once step 3 has been completed, store the 4 larger pods in a plastic bag.

Brush the bottom of the wired pod with edible glue and press 2 of the larger pods against it, opposite one another (step 4). Repeat for the remaining centres and leave them to set for at least 30 minutes.

Once set, attach another 2 pods in between the first pair. Repeat for the remaining centres and leave to dry overnight.

Once dry, brush the tips of the peony centres with deep magenta petal dust (step 5).

MAKING THE STAMEN

Using tweezers, make an open hook at one end of each 26-gauge wire.

Divide the 3 bunches of stamen in half and bundle each set together with the hooked wire. Bend the stamen upwards in the middle (step 6) and fan them out (step 7). Brush the stamen generously with primrose petal dust.

Arrange the stamen underneath the peony centre and tape them together using green florist tape (step 8).

MAKING THE PETALS

You will need 18 petals per peony; 6 of each shape (step 9). Roll out some pink flower paste on a veining board, to a thickness of 1mm.

Flip over the paste. Select cutter number 1 and place it on the paste with the petal tip over the thickest part of the vein. Cut out the petal (step 10).

Place the petal on a foam mat and ball the edges with a Celpin (see page 217).

Dip the end of a white 26-gauge wire in edible glue and insert it into the base of the vein, about one-third of the way into the petal.

Flatten the vein on the back of the petal and turn it over.

Press the peony petal veiner onto the petal (step 11).

Pinch the bottom of the petal along the wire, and bend the wire up slightly.

Curl back the petal edges using a small Celstick, holding the petal with 1 finger over the stick, then stretching and rolling back the paste a little (step 12). It is important to stretch the paste, otherwise the edges will bounce back.

Place the petal on a perforated foam mat and bend the wire upwards.

Repeat this process to make the other 35 petals using the same cutter. Repeat for 36 petals each using the other 2 petal cutters.

Leave the petals to dry overnight.

DUSTING THE FLOWERS

Dust the petals with a blend of fuchsia, strawberry and a little poppy red petal dust. Brush from the outer edge of each petal to the centre, on the back and front, letting it fade out towards the bottom (step 13).

TAPING THE FLOWERS

Using tweezers, space out the stamen evenly.

Sharply bend the wire of each peony petal downwards at an angle of 90°.

Arrange the first layer of 6 petals (made with cutter number 1) evenly around the centre and tape them to the stem one by one (step 14).

Arrange the next layer of 6 petals (made with cutter number 2) underneath and in between the first layer, taping them in place as above (step 15). Finally, attach the last layer of 6 petals (made with cutter number 3) in the same way (step 16).

Wind the tape all the way down the stem and trim the end with wire scissors. Repeat the process for the remaining peonies.

STEAMING THE FLOWERS

Steam each peony for about 3 seconds to set the colours and give them a satin-like sheen.

MAKING THE LEAVES

Mix about 100g of white flower paste with gooseberry food paste colour to make a light green shade. Wrap the paste in a plastic bag and let it rest for about 15 minutes.

Roll out the paste on a veining board to a thickness of about 1mm.

Cut out a leaf shape using the peony leaf cutter, with the thicker part of the vein centred at the base.

Place the leaf on a foam pad, dip the end of a 26-gauge wire in edible glue and insert it into the base of the leaf vein, about one-third of the way into the vein.

Gently ball the edges of the leaf with a Celpin (step 17).

Place the leaf on the base of the peony leaf veiner and press down the top of the veiner to emboss (step 18).

Lift the leaf off the veiner and pinch the paste at the top and bottom of the leaf.

Place the leaf on a perforated foam mat and leave it to dry (step 19).

Repeat the process to make another 5 leaves.

Once dry, dust the leaves with a blend of holly and spring green petal dust, brushing from the edges to the middle and from the base upwards (step 20).

Wind green florist tape around the wires, then steam the leaves for about 3 seconds to set the colour and give them a satin-like sheen.

TO DECORATE THE CAKE

Poke holes in the icing, large enough for the flower picks, using the end of an artist's paintbrush (step 21).

Using tweezers, insert the stems into plastic flower picks (step 22) and push them into the cake tiers (step 23). To achieve the best result, work your way down from the top tier, spacing the largest flowers out first, then filling the gaps with the smaller flowers.

Bend the wires into shape, trying to cover any gaps (step 24). It is always a good idea to have some extra single blossoms and leaves to fill small spaces. If you wish, you could put a dab of royal icing onto the backs of the flowers to secure them.

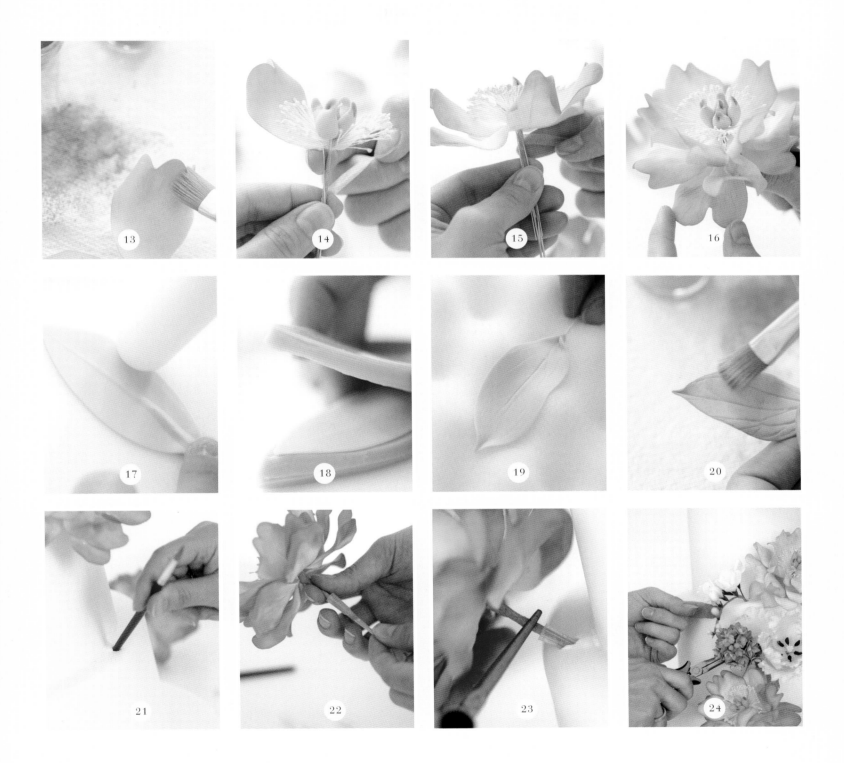

BAKING & ICING BASICS

PLANNING AHEAD

One of the questions I am asked most often is, 'How soon should I start making my cake?' While fruit cakes can be baked and iced several weeks in advance, layered sponge cakes require careful planning in order to ensure that the cake is as fresh as possible without compromising its shape and structure. Once a sponge cake is covered with marzipan and sugar paste it will stay fresh and moist for longer, without the need for refrigeration, as long as the filling doesn't contain raw eggs or fresh cream. As a rule of thumb, my advice is to work to a 5-day plan for tiered cakes, to allow enough resting and setting time in between each stage:

day 1 Bake sponges and make sugar syrup if required; start flower decorations if time.

day 2 Make cake fillings and layer cakes; continue flower decorations if time.

day 3 Cover cakes with marzipan; continue flower decorations.

day 4 Ice cakes and cake board with sugar paste; finish flower decorations.

day 5 Dowel and stack cake tiers and cake board; arrange flowers on cake and finish the design. Allow a tiered cake to set for at least 4 hours before transportation.

BASIC RECIPES

Although the main focus of this book is on making beautiful sugar flowers, I strongly believe that a cake needs to taste as good as it looks. The following recipes have been tried and tested in our kitchens over many years and provide a perfect base for iced cakes that will stack well and are strong enough to hold up decorations such as sugar flowers. You can use one flavour for all tiers or flavour each tier differently. The main thing to consider if you choose to do the latter, is the density and strength of each flavour. The strongest cake, able to carry the most weight, is the luxury fruit cake (see page 202), followed by the rich dark chocolate cake (see page 201). However, there is no reason why you couldn't use the chocolate cake as a bottom tier, a sponge in the middle and a small fruit cake for the top tier. If you are a more adventurous baker, use my list of cake flavour combinations (see page 203) as a starting point and refine them to suit your own taste. On the page opposite is a list of basic baking tools that I consider essentials for making cakes in the home kitchen.

BAKING TOOL KIT

Selection of cake tins and baking trays
Electric mixer with paddle attachment
Rubber spatula
Selection of bowls and jugs
Flour sieve
Kitchen scales
Greaseproof paper
Spray oil
Cupcake liners (for cupcakes only)
Plastic piping bag (for cupcakes only)
Step palette knife
Pastry brush
Scissors
Wire cooling rack
Small kitchen knife
Whisk
Oven gloves
Microplane grater (for grating zests only)

LINING A CAKE TIN

When choosing cake tins, I have discovered that you will get a more evenly baked sponge in a shallower tin. For sponge cakes and chocolate cakes I use tins with a depth of 4–5cm. For fruit cakes I use deeper tins but insulate the sides with a thick layer of greaseproof paper, as this will prevent the cake from burning around the edges.
Line your tins using the following method:

Place the cake tin on a sheet of greaseproof paper and draw a line around the base with a pencil.

Cut out the shape on the inside of the line with scissors.

To line the sides of the tin, cut out a strip of greaseproof paper that is about 5cm higher than the depth of the tin and long enough to line the inside edge. For large tins you can join 2 strips together.

Once cut, fold the strip lengthways, 2.5cm from the top, and make little cuts along the edge, up to the crease.

Lightly spray the inside of the tin with oil and place the strip of paper around the sides with the snipped edge down and the snips facing towards the middle of the tin.

Place the paper base inside, over the snipped edge, to form a flat base with sharp corners. This will ensure that the cake mix won't leak through the paper during baking. For a square tin, fold the long paper strip at the 4 corners so that it fits neatly inside the tin.

VICTORIA SPONGE

My Victoria sponge recipe is based on the simple principle of using equal quantities of butter, sugar, eggs and flour. The key to its success is – as with all baking – using the freshest and best-quality ingredients available and to follow the technique in the recipe down to the finest detail. Baking is all about being well prepared and having patience.

Makes enough to fill three 15cm-diameter tins or one 25cm-diameter sandwich cake tin 4cm deep;
a 30 x 20cm baking tray (for miniature cakes) or 20–24 cupcakes.
For other sizes and quantities, please refer to the guide on page 218.
Baking temperature: 180°C, gas mark 4
Baking time: 12–15 minutes for cupcakes; 20–45 minutes for large cakes, depending on size.

INGREDIENTS
200g salted butter (or unsalted with a pinch of salt), softened
200g caster sugar
4 medium eggs, at room temperature
200g self-raising flour, sifted
100ml sugar syrup (see page 204)

OPTIONAL FLAVOURS
For vanilla sponge, add the seeds of 1 vanilla pod and 1 teaspoon vanilla extract
For lemon sponge, add the finely grated zest of 3 unwaxed lemons
For orange sponge, add the finely grated zest of 2 unwaxed oranges

Preheat the oven to 180°C/gas mark 4. Line the cake tin with greaseproof paper as described on page 197. For cupcakes, place paper cases in muffin tins.

Place the butter, caster sugar and flavouring of your choice in an electric mixer and, using the paddle, beat at medium–high speed until pale and fluffy.

Beat the eggs lightly in a separate bowl or jug and slowly pour into the butter mixture while paddling on medium speed. If the mixture starts to curdle, add a handful of flour to bring it back together.

Once the butter, sugar and eggs are combined, mix in the flour at low speed until it is just combined.

Using a rubber spatula, fold through the batter to make sure everything is fully mixed in.

For large cakes, transfer the batter to the lined tin and gently spread it towards the edges with a step palette knife. The mix should be higher around the edges of the tin and dipped down in the middle, as this will ensure a more even bake and cake height.

For cupcakes, put the batter into a large piping bag, snip about 2.5cm off the bottom and fill the paper cases to about two-thirds full.

Bake for 20–45 minutes for large cakes and 12–15 minutes for cupcakes. The sponge is cooked when it springs back to the touch and the sides are coming away from the edges of the tin. Alternatively, insert the clean blade of

a knife into the middle of the sponge; if it is cooked, the knife will come out clean.

Once cooked, leave the cake (or cakes) to rest in the tin for about 10 minutes before removing and placing on a wire rack to cool.

While the sponge is still hot, brush the top with the sugar syrup; this will add moisture and stop the top from becoming hard and crusty.

Once cool, wrap the sponge in clingfilm and store in a cool dry place overnight. This will allow the crumb to rest and firm up a little, making it ideal for layering the next day. Cupcakes should be used fresh on the day of baking.

RICH DARK CHOCOLATE CAKE

This chocolate cake recipe is a little more moist than others, but it is also denser and heavier, which makes it an excellent base for tiered and iced celebration cakes. This cake has a shelf life of up to 10 days after icing.

Makes enough to fill three 15cm-diameter tins or one 25cm-diameter sandwich cake tin 4cm deep;
a 30 x 20cm baking tray (for miniature cakes) or 20–24 cupcakes.
For other sizes and quantities, please refer to the guide on page 216.
Baking temperature: 160°C, gas mark 3
Baking time: about 15 minutes for cupcakes; 20–45 minutes for large cakes, depending on size

INGREDIENTS

100g salted butter (or unsalted with a pinch of salt), softened
340g brown sugar
100g plain chocolate drops (53% cocoa solids)
150ml milk
3 medium eggs, lightly beaten, at room temperature — *Separate & whisk whites*
225g plain flour, sifted
2¼ tablespoons cocoa powder
¾ teaspoon bicarbonate of soda
¾ teaspoon baking powder

Preheat the oven to 160°C/gas mark 3. Line the cake tin as described on page 197. For cupcakes, place paper cases in muffin tins.

Using an electric mixer with a paddle attachment, beat the butter and half of the sugar until pale and fluffy.

Meanwhile, place the chocolate, milk and remaining sugar in a deep pan and bring to the boil, stirring occasionally.

Once the butter and sugar mixture is pale and fluffy, slowly add the eggs. *yolks*

Sift together the flour, cocoa powder, bicarbonate of soda and baking powder

and add to the mixture while ~~mixing on slow speed.~~ *folding.*

Pour the hot chocolate mixture into a jug, then slowly pour it into the cake batter while mixing on slow speed. Take care, as the hot mixture could splash back at you. *Add egg whites*

Once combined, pour the hot cake batter into the prepared tin or transfer to a jug and pour the batter into cupcake cases, filling them to about two-thirds full.

Bake for 20–45 minutes for a large cake or 15 minutes for cupcakes. The sponge is cooked when it springs back to the touch and the sides are coming away from the edges of the tin.

Alternatively, insert the clean blade of a knife into the middle of the sponge; if it is cooked, the knife will come out clean.

Once cooked, let the cake (or cakes) rest for about 10 minutes in the tin before removing and placing on a wire rack to cool.

Once cool, wrap the cake with clingfilm and store in a cool dry place overnight. This will allow the crumb to rest and firm up a little, making it ideal for layering the next day. Cupcakes should be used fresh on the day of baking.

LUXURY FRUIT CAKE

This is a light, moist fruit cake with a slight crunch from the dried figs. Bake the cake several days to a week in advance to allow it to rest and fully develop its fruity flavours. If you wish, you could make it several weeks, if not months, in advance. For extra moisture and a boozy flavour, keep feeding the cake with whisky on a weekly basis and store it wrapped in greaseproof paper and foil in a cool dry place until ready to ice.

Makes one round 15cm-diameter fruit cake baked in a 7.5cm-deep cake tin.
Baking temperature: 140°C, gas mark 1
Baking time: 2–3 hours

INGREDIENTS

For the fruit mix
(make one day in advance)
150g raisins
65g dried cranberries, halved
230g sultanas, roughly chopped
120g whole glacé cherries, chopped
80g dried figs, chopped
60ml whisky
50g golden syrup
Grated zest of 1 unwaxed lemon

For the cake mix
120g eggs (about 2 small eggs)
90g dark brown sugar
115g unsalted butter, softened
25g ground almonds
90g plain flour, sifted
¼ teaspoon ground cinnamon
Pinch of ground cloves
Pinch of ground nutmeg
Pinch of salt
30ml whisky, for soaking

Place all the ingredients for the fruit mix in a large bowl, stir well and cover with clingfilm. Leave to infuse overnight at room temperature.

The next day, preheat the oven to 140°C/ gas mark 1. Line the cake tin with greaseproof paper as described on page 197.

Place the eggs and sugar in a medium bowl and whisk by hand until combined.

In a separate bowl, cream together the butter and ground almonds until just creamy but not too aerated.

Slowly add the egg mixture until you have a smooth emulsion. If the mixture starts to curdle,

add a handful of flour to rebind the batter. Sift together the remaining dry ingredients and fold through the batter in 2 batches until just combined.

Add the infused fruit to the cake batter and combine thoroughly and evenly, then pour the cake mixture into the prepared tin and level the surface with the back of a spoon. Tap the filled cake tin on your work surface to tap out any air bubbles and to ensure that the batter has reached all the corners at the bottom of the tin.

Insulate the sides of the cake tin with a strip of greaseproof paper folded several times; hold it in place with a piece of string.

Bake on a low shelf in the oven for 2–3 hours. To prevent the cake from browning too much on the top, place an oven tray on the shelf above the cake tin. The cake is cooked when the top is golden brown. If in doubt, insert a clean knife into the centre of the cake; if it is cooked, the knife will come out clean.

Allow the cake to cool for about 10 minutes, then, while still warm, brush the top of the cake generously with the whisky. Leave the cake to cool completely on a wire rack before wrapping it in greaseproof paper and foil.

ENGLISH BUTTERCREAM

Following a traditional recipe, this buttercream is based on the principle of using equal quantities of butter and icing sugar. The method is very simple, and the sugar quantity can be increased to double the amount of butter in order to give a large tiered cake more stability during hot summer months. As this recipe is egg-free, the buttercream has a shelf life of at least 2 weeks if kept in the fridge, and an iced cake layered with this buttercream doesn't need to be refrigerated once it has been covered with marzipan and sugar paste. Ideally, make the buttercream fresh before use, as this is when it has the perfect texture and consistency for layering.

Makes 400g, roughly the amount needed to sandwich and mask three 15cm-diameter layers of sponge cake. For other sizes and quantities, please refer to the quantity guide on page 218.

INGREDIENTS
200g unsalted butter, softened
200g icing sugar
Pinch of salt

OPTIONAL FLAVOURS
For vanilla buttercream
Add 1 teaspoon vanilla extract or seeds of 1 vanilla pod
For lemon buttercream
Add the finely grated zest of 2 unwaxed lemons
For orange buttercream
Add the finely grated zest of 2 unwaxed oranges

Place the butter, icing sugar, salt and optional flavouring in an electric mixer with a paddle attachment. Bring the mixture together on low speed, then increase to medium–high speed and beat until the mixture becomes pale and fluffy. If not using immediately, transfer the buttercream to an airtight container and store in the fridge. Remove from the fridge 1–2 hours before using, to allow it to come back to room temperature.

GANACHE

Makes 400g, roughly the amount needed to sandwich three 15cm-diameter layers of chocolate cake. For other sizes and quantities, please refer to the quantity guide on page 218.

INGREDIENTS
200g plain Belgian chocolate drops (I use those with 53% cocoa solids)
200ml single cream

Place the chocolate drops in a deep bowl.

Pour the cream into a deep pan and bring to a simmer.

Pour the cream over the chocolate drops and whisk gently until the chocolate has melted and the mixture is smooth.

Leave to cool until just setting before use. It can be stored in an airtight container in the fridge for up to a month.

CAKE FILLINGS & FLAVOUR COMBINATIONS

To make a classic Victoria sponge, sandwich 3 layers of vanilla sponge with 1 layer of vanilla buttercream and 1 layer of luxury strawberry or raspberry preserve.

To make a delicious and refreshing lemon cake, mix the buttercream with lemon curd or my lemon limoncello jelly, to taste. Sandwich 3 layers of lemon sponge with the lemon buttercream.

To make a fragrant moist orange cake, sandwich 3 layers of orange sponge with 1 layer of orange buttercream and 1 layer of luxury orange marmalade. Alternatively, use my orange and Grand Marnier marmalade.

To make a chocolate and orange cake, sandwich 3 layers of orange sponge with 1 layer of Belgian chocolate ganache and 1 layer of orange marmalade.

For a rich dark chocolate cake, sandwich 3 layers of rich dark chocolate sponge with 2 layers of Belgian chocolate ganache.

CAKE LAYERING

In this section I will demonstrate, step by step, how to layer a cake tier using several layers of sponge or chocolate cake filled with either buttercream and preserves (optional) or ganache and soaked with syrup (where required). Most of my tiered cakes are made up of 3 cake layers and 2 layers of filling, with a tier height of 10cm. However, some of the designs in this book require tiers of different sizes, so please read the instructions carefully and refer to the guide on page 218, as the quantity of filling required will depend on the flavour, size and shape of cake you wish to make. Below is a list of tools that I find incredible helpful when layering cakes.

LAYERING TOOL KIT

Long serrated knife or cake leveller (whichever you find easier to work with)

Ruler that measures in inches

Cake drum or thick cake board (for the base of large cakes)

Large palette knife

Small palette knife

Pastry brush

Non-slip turntable

Metal disc (the one I use is about 30cm in diameter from Alan Silverwood. I use it as a base to layer cakes on)

Metal side scraper

Greaseproof paper

Round pastry cutter set (for miniature cakes)

Small cake cards (for miniature cakes)

SUGAR SYRUP

Makes 100ml, roughly the amount needed for a 15cm-diameter layered cake tier or 20–24 cupcakes

INGREDIENTS

75ml water

75g caster sugar

OPTIONAL FLAVOURS

1 teaspoon vanilla extract

Juice of 1 lemon

Juice of 1 orange

Place the water, flavouring if using, and the sugar into a pan and bring
to the boil. Remove from the heat and allow to cool. You can store the
syrup in an airtight container in the fridge for up to a month.

LAYERING MINIATURE CAKES

INGREDIENTS

For 12 miniature round cakes (5cm in diameter x 5cm high)

20 x 30cm rectangular cake layer (if you haven't got a suitably sized baking tray, you can use a 25cm square cake tin instead)

About 1kg ganache or buttercream (see page 203)

100ml sugar syrup, for sponge cake only (see below left)

EQUIPMENT

5cm-diameter round pastry cutter

12 x 5cm-diameter cake cards

Cake layering tool kit (see left)

Trim the top crust off the cake using a long serrated knife or cake leveller (step 1). The height of the cake should be just over 2.5cm.

Cut circles out of the cake using the round pastry cutter.

Spread out 12 cake cards on your work surface (one per mini cake) and spread a small dab of ganache or buttercream in the centre of each one.

Place 1 cake circle, crust facing downwards, on each cake card (step 2). If using, soak the top of each cake with a little sugar syrup.

Spread the cake filling over the top and place the next cake circle on top, crust facing up this time (step 3). Gently press down to push out any air bubbles. If using, brush the tops lightly with sugar syrup.

Place all the cakes on a small tray and wrap with clingfilm, then chill in the fridge until the cakes and fillings are firm.

Once chilled, take a few cakes out at a time (I usually take about 6). Mask the cakes by covering them thinly with buttercream or ganache using a small palette knife (step 4). Try to keep the tops and sides as even and smooth as possible. Don't worry if a few gaps are showing the crumb. Miniature cakes are much more forgiving than large cakes.

Once masked, put the cakes back on the tray and chill in the fridge until the coating has set and the cakes are firm.

1

2

3

4

LAYERING LARGE CAKES

INGREDIENTS
For a 15cm-diameter round cake tier, about 10cm high
3 x 15cm-diameter round cake layers
About 350g buttercream, jam or ganache (see page 203)
100ml sugar syrup, for sponge cake only (see page 204)

EQUIPMENT
15cm-diameter round cake drum
Cake layering tool kit (see page 204)

Trim the tops and bottoms off your cake layers using a cake leveller (step 1) or long serrated knife (step 2). Ensure that each layer is level and straight and about the same height – ideally, just over 2.5cm.

Place your cake drum on the turntable, then spread a dab of buttercream, jam or ganache in the middle of the drum (step 3). Lay the first cake layer on top, making sure the sides are flush with the drum.

If you are using sponge cake and it feels a little dry after trimming, brush the surface lightly with sugar syrup. I generally soak sponge cakes to give them extra moisture and flavour.

Spread the first cake layer evenly with buttercream or ganache. The filling should be 3–5mm thick (step 4).

Centre the next cake layer on top and brush the surface with sugar syrup if necessary. Add buttercream or ganache as before (steps 5–6), then add the final layer.

Brush a little sugar syrup over the last cake layer (if using sponge cake).

Once all the layers are assembled, gently press the top down to ensure that any trapped air bubbles are released and the top is level.

Pile a generous amount of buttercream or ganache on top (step 7) and spread it evenly over the top (step 8) and down the sides (steps 9–10) to mask the cake. Use a side scraper to clean up the sides (step 11) and a long palette knife to clean the top (step 12). Try to make the top edge of the cake as sharp and clean as possible.

Chill the cake in the fridge for about 2 hours, to set the first coat.

Most cakes benefit from a second coating after the first has set, in order to perfect the shape and seal any gaps. If this is the case with your cake, repeat steps 7–12 and chill the cake again overnight. If you have managed to achieve a nice even cake shape with the first coat, let the cake chill overnight until firm.

ICING CAKES WITH MARZIPAN & SUGAR PASTE

After baking and layering, icing cakes is probably the most basic and essential skill required in cake making and sugarcraft. Once the materials and techniques are understood, it is all about practice. The more cakes you ice, the better the finishes will be.

ICING TOOL KIT

Small icing sugar sieve
Large rolling pin
Pair of marzipan spacers
Pair of cake smoothers
Kitchen knife
Round pastry cutter (for miniature cakes only)
Scriber pin

tips Here are a few general tips that you need to know before getting started:

Always cover cakes from chilled, except for fruit cakes. This will ensure that the cake holds its shape, allowing you to use a little more pressure when icing it.

Always knead marzipan or sugar paste on a clean smooth work surface, without icing sugar, unless the paste is very sticky and you need to change the consistency. Adding icing sugar makes marzipan or sugar paste dryer and, if used too much, can result in little cracks and tears on the surface, which we call 'stretch marks' or 'elephant skin'.

Remove any rings you might be wearing and be careful with your fingertips. Use cake smoothers or a palette knife where possible when moving or lifting an iced cake, to avoid leaving any marks on the icing.

After covering a cake with marzipan, always let it set overnight before icing it with sugar paste. This will allow the marzipan to harden and the cake to hold its shape well.

Brushing marzipan with clear alcohol will create a natural adhesive that also sterilises the surface. Don't worry about taste, as the alcohol will evaporate quickly. If you don't wish to use alcohol, use cool boiled water instead.

Should any air bubbles appear in the icing, poke them with a sterile scriber pin and push the air out with your fingers. Air bubbles often appear a few hours after icing, once the cake has had time to come to room temperature and the sponge layers have started to shrink ever so slightly. Go back to look at your cake tier from time to time, to make sure that you get rid of any air bubbles before the icing hardens.

ICING LARGE CHOCOLATE OR SPONGE CAKES

INGREDIENTS
Chilled layered sponge or chocolate cake tier
Marzipan (for quantity, use the guide on page 218)
Sugar paste (for quantity, use the guide on page 218)
Icing sugar, for dusting
Clear alcohol, such as vodka (or cool boiled water)

EQUIPMENT
Icing tool kit (see page 209)

Remove the cake from the fridge and place it on a sheet of greaseproof paper a few centimetres wider than the cake base. While you roll out the marzipan, the outside of the cake will naturally become a little sticky through condensation building up on the surface. Therefore, there is no need to cover the cake with more buttercream or ganache.

Knead the marzipan into a smooth ball to make it more pliable. If the texture is very sticky, knead in some icing sugar until the marzipan becomes more paste-like.

Dust a clean smooth work surface with a generous layer of icing sugar. Place the marzipan in the centre with a marzipan spacer either side of the ball.

Using a large non-stick rolling pin, roll out the marzipan to an even thickness of about 5mm, making sure that the width and depth is large enough to cover the cake in one piece. Should any air bubbles appear in the marzipan, prick them with the scriber pin and push out the air.

Flip the marzipan sheet over the rolling pin, dust off any excess icing sugar underneath, and lift the marzipan over the cake. Some people prefer to use their hands; however, I find that by using the rolling pin to lift the sheet, you get fewer fingerprints and stretch marks in your marzipan.

Once the marzipan is lying over the cake, flatten the top using the smoothers.

Next, use your palms to push the marzipan against the edges at the top of the cake (step 1, opposite). Then, gently use the flat parts of your hands to push the marzipan all the way down the sides (step 2). As marzipan is very flexible, you can stretch it out a little if it's not quite long enough to reach the bottom edge of the cake. Use one hand to unfold any creases around the bottom and the other to push the marzipan flat against the sides of the cake.

Once you have reached the bottom edge, tuck the marzipan into the corners, first with your hands then with the straight edge of a smoother.

Trim off the excess marzipan with a long straight-edged kitchen knife or palette knife (step 3). Make sure you cut straight down and not at an angle towards the cake, as this will create a gap underneath the marzipan.

Using both smoothers, with the straight edges facing down towards the table, run them over the marzipan as though you are ironing a piece of clothing. Polish and smooth the top and sides until you have an even surface (step 4). If you need to turn and move your cake around in order to reach all the sides, use the paper underneath to pull it into the required position. This way, you don't have to touch the surface with your fingers and risk leaving marks.

Once finished, I like to let the marzipan layer set and firm up overnight at room temperature. In particular for tiered and large cakes, this will enhance the stability and structure of the cake.

Once set, check the cake for any air bubbles. At this stage you are still able to prick them and push the air out, as the marzipan will still be flexible.

Brush the marzipan thinly with the alcohol or water, making sure not to create any puddles around the base of the cake. Repeat the entire process using sugar paste instead of marzipan.

ICING LARGE FRUIT CAKES

INGREDIENTS
Smooth apricot jam
Fruit cake (see page 202)
Marzipan (for quantity, use the guide on page 218)
Sugar paste (for quantity, use the guide on page 218)
Icing sugar, for dusting
Clear alcohol, such as vodka (or use cool boiled water)

EQUIPMENT
Cake drum of the same size as the cake base
Icing tool kit (see page 209)

Spread a thin layer of apricot jam over the centre of the cake drum and place the cake on top with the top facing down.

Roll some of the marzipan into a thin sausage and push it into the gap between the cake and the cake drum, making sure the sides are flush. Most fruit cakes will have a few little holes all across the surface from sunken fruits, so roll tiny balls of marzipan to fill them so the surface is as even as possible. You can also rebuild the edge of a cake using this technique, if it hasn't turned out sharp enough. This can happen when the cake mixture doesn't spread into the bottom corners of the cake tin properly.

Bring the apricot jam to the boil and whisk carefully until smooth. If the jam is a little thick, add some water. Take care, as jam can bubble up and burn your hands if it is very hot.

Place the cake on a sheet of greaseproof paper a few centimetres wider than the cake base. Using a pastry brush, coat the outside of the cake (including the sides of the cake drum) thinly with the jam.

Cover the cake with marzipan and sugar paste following the instructions for chocolate or sponge cakes (see opposite).

1

2

3

4

ICING MINIATURE CAKES

INGREDIENTS

Marzipan (for quantity, use the guide on page 218)

Icing sugar, for dusting

Masked, chilled miniature cakes or mini fruit cakes (for quantity, use the guide on page 218)

Smooth apricot jam, boiled and cooled slightly (for fruit cakes only)

Clear alcohol, such as vodka (or use cool boiled water)

Sugar paste (for quantities, use the guide on page 218)

EQUIPMENT

Icing tool kit (page 209)

Cake cards (for fruit cakes only)

Knead the marzipan into a smooth ball to make it more pliable. If the texture is very sticky, knead in some icing sugar until the marzipan becomes more paste-like.

Dust a clean smooth work surface with a generous layer of icing sugar and place the marzipan in the middle. Using a large non-stick rolling pin, roll out the marzipan to an even thickness of about 3–4mm. If any air bubbles appear, prick them with the scriber pin and push out the air.

Using a small plain kitchen knife, cut out squares of marzipan, each large enough to cover one miniature cake (step 1). Cut out as many pieces at once as you can. With a little icing sugar dusted in between, pile them on top of each other.

If covering sponge cakes, take 4–6 miniature cakes from the fridge and place them on a surface lightly dusted with icing sugar. For fruit cakes, put your cakes upside down on a small cake card with a dab of apricot jam underneath. If necessary, fill any holes in the cakes with small balls of marzipan, then brush the surface thinly with hot apricot jam.

Place a piece of marzipan over the top of each cake (step 2), flatten the tops with a smoother and push the sides down with your hands. Be careful not to tear the marzipan around the edges of the cakes.

Once you have reached the bottom edge, tuck the marzipan right into the corners, first with your hands, then with the straight edge of a smoother. Trim off the excess marzipan with

a small plain-edged knife or a round pastry cutter that fits just around the cake (step 3).

Hold the smoothers so the straight edges face down towards the table, then run them over the marzipan (step 4). Polish and smooth the top and sides until the surface is even. Let the marzipan layer set and firm up overnight at room temperature.

Once rested, check the cake for any air bubbles. At this stage, you will still be able to prick them and push the air out, as the marzipan will still be flexible.

Brush the marzipan thinly with the alcohol or water, taking care not to create any puddles around the base of the cake. Repeat the process using sugar paste instead of marzipan.

1

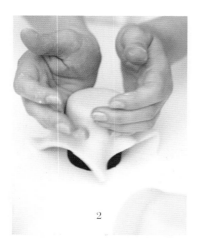

2

3

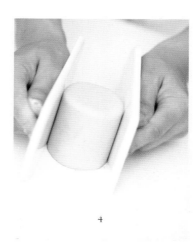

4

ICING A CAKE BOARD

Ice your cake board at least 1–2 days ahead, to ensure that the icing
has dried properly before placing a cake on top.

INGREDIENTS

Sugar paste (for quantity, use the guide on page 218)
Icing sugar, for dusting

EQUIPMENT

Cake drum of the required size and shape
15mm-wide satin ribbon, long enough to cover the edge of the cake board
Double-sided sticky tape
Icing tool kit (page 209)

Brush the cake board thinly with water.

Knead the sugar paste into a smooth ball, place it on a smooth work surface dusted with icing sugar and roll it out to an even thickness of about 3mm, making sure it is large enough to overlap the edges of the cake drum.

Flip the sheet of sugar paste over your rolling pin and lay it onto the cake drum (step 1).

Trim any small pieces of sugar paste off the sides of the board with a clean plain-edged kitchen knife (step 2). Leave about 1cm overlapping the sides. Pull the iced board to the edge of your work surface and push the overlapping sugar paste down the sides with the smoothers at a 45° angle, until it falls off.

Run over the top with a cake smoother to polish the surface. If there are any air bubbles in the icing, prick them with a scriber pin and push the air out with the smoother (step 3).

Smooth the edges by running the smoothers sideways in a downward motion, to create a chamfered edge (step 4). Again, work in a downward motion to ensure that the paste doesn't lift up around the edges of the board. Leave the iced board to dry.

Once the paste is dry, stick a few pieces of double-sided sticky tape around the edges and attach the ribbon tightly. Overlap the ends by about 1cm and fix them together with another piece of tape.

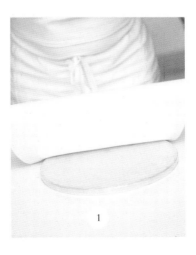

DOWELLING & STACKING TIERED CAKES

Dowelling a cake means inserting pillars into the cake centre to support the weight of the tier or tiers above. I prefer hollow dowel rods as they are wider and easier to cut to the required height than some types of dowel, but you can also opt for thin plastic dowels or – for smaller, lighter cakes – even straws. Always dowel and stack your cake tiers at least half a day before transporting them, or, even better, a day in advance, otherwise the royal icing that is holding the tiers in place might not be dry and the cake could slide during transportation. Below is a list of the tools required for dowelling and stacking cakes. You will also need royal icing to stick the cake tiers together. Use it as freshly made as possible as it will stick better than icing that is a few days old.

DOWELLING & STACKING TOOL KIT

Large palette knife
Dowelling template (optional)
Small serrated kitchen knife
Edible pen or scriber pin (optional)
Hollow plastic dowels (or other type according
to your preference)
Scissors
Cake smoother
Small spirit level (optional)
Spare cake drum, large enough to overlap the dowels
on the bottom tier

Using the palette knife, spread a thin layer of royal icing in the centre of the iced cake board (step 1).

Carefully lift the iced bottom tier off the paper and centre it on the cake board (step 2).

With the template (if using), mark the positions of the 4 dowels. Dowels should always sit as close to the outside of the cake as possible, for maximum stability, but they shouldn't show or sit further out than the cake board underneath the tier that will be placed on top.

Mark these positions with an edible pen or a scriber pin (step 3).

Remove the template, find the mark for the first dowel and carefully push it down through the cake until it hits the drum (step 4). I tend to twist the dowel as I push, as I find this prevents the icing around it from cracking too much.

Mark the dowel about 1mm above the surface of the cake and pull it out carefully. Mark the 3 remaining dowels at the same point using the mark on the first dowel as a guide.

Cut the excess length off each dowel using the serrated knife. Tidy up the edges with a pair of scissors if necessary (step 5).

Double-check that all the dowels are exactly the same length, then push them into the cake at the 4 points you marked in step 3 (step 6). The dowels should all stick out of the cake by about 1mm (step 7).

Place a spare cake drum on top of the 4 dowels and push down with an even pressure. Use the spirit level to check that the dowels are level. If they're not, figure out which one needs trimming, pull it out and cut it a little shorter. Never cut the dowels shorter than the height of the cake; otherwise the weight of the tier above will crack the icing of the cake below.

Next, dowel the remaining tiers, except for the top one. Centre the cakes on top of each other with a layer of royal icing in between to hold them together (steps 8–9).

ROYAL ICING

Royal icing is an essential ingredient for cake decorating and sugarcraft, and I use it for most of the cake designs in this book, whether it is to make piped decorations such as dots, flower centres and lace, or as a strong glue to hold cake tiers and decorations together. For professional purposes I would recommend using dried egg white, also called Meri-white, rather than fresh. However, for private use you can simply replace the amount of Meri-white indicated with fresh egg white. As a general rule, the ratio of icing sugar to liquid should be 6 to 1.

INGREDIENTS

1kg icing sugar, sifted
25g Meri-white, mixed with about 165ml water
(check the instructions on the packet,
as the ratio may differ between brands),
or 4 medium egg whites
Squeeze of lemon juice (optional)

EQUIPMENT

Electric mixer with paddle attachment
Storage container with lid or clingfilm
J-cloth

Place the icing sugar in the clean bowl of an electric mixer. Pour in about three-quarters of the Meri-white mix or egg whites and the lemon juice (if using). The use of lemon juice is optional; its purpose is to strengthen the albumen in the egg. Mix together on low speed for about 2 minutes. If the mixture looks too dry and crumbly, add the remaining Meri-white or egg whites until the mixture looks smooth but not wet. Stop mixing and scrape the sides and base of the bowl with a rubber spatula, then turn the mixer back on at a low speed.

Keep mixing on low speed, keeping an eye on the consistency by checking the icing along the sides of the bowl. It should look smooth but almost dry with a satin-like sheen. As the paddle keeps turning, you will notice the icing stiffening and beginning to form peaks that stand away from the edges of the bowl. If you hear a swishing sound (which is from the air in the icing being moved around) that is becoming louder, the icing is almost ready.

After about 5 minutes, do a test by dipping a clean rubber spatula or spoon into the icing and holding it up in the air. If the icing holds up in a stiff peak, the icing is ready. If the peak flops over, keep mixing it for another minute or so until it has reached a stiff-peak consistency.

Transfer the royal icing to a clean sealable plastic container and cover it with a damp clean cloth before sealing it with a lid or wrapping it in clingfilm. The icing can be stored at room temperature for about a week; however, for best results, I recommend using it as freshly made as possible.

ROYAL ICING CONSISTENCIES

Throughout this book, I refer to two different consistencies of royal icing: stiff peak and soft peak.

stiff-peak icing is used for sticking cake tiers together and attaching flowers to cakes, as it is the strongest consistency. As the name suggests, the icing forms a stiff peak when lifted with a spoon or palette knife. It doesn't usually require any additional water unless the icing is a few days old or too dry. When freshly made, you can take it straight from the container and put it into a piping bag, or use it as required. If the icing is a few days old, soften it with a palette knife before putting it into a piping bag.

soft-peak icing is used for piping fine dots and lines onto cakes and into the centres of flowers, for example. You can make it by adding a little water to your stiff-peak icing and softening it with a small palette knife. If adding colour, always mix the food colour through first with a palette knife, then add the water. Soft-peak icing should look slightly glossy with the peak falling over, without spreading out.

MAKING A PAPER PIPING BAG

Take a rectangle of greaseproof paper (about 30 x 45cm) and cut it in half diagonally from corner to corner. Rather than snipping, slide the blades of the scissors through the paper to make a cleaner cut.

Hold one of the resulting paper triangles with one hand in the middle of the longest side and the other on the point on the opposite side. The longer side of the triangle should be on your left.

Curl the shorter corner on your right over to the corner that is pointing towards you, so it forms a cone (step 1).

With your left hand, wrap the longer corner on the left around the tip of the cone twice (step 2).

Join the corner with the other 2 corners at the back of the cone (step 3).

If the piping bag has an open tip at the front, close it by wiggling the inner and outer layers back and forth until the cone forms a sharp point.

Fold the corners at the open end into the inside of the bag twice, to prevent it from unravelling (step 4).

Only half-fill the bag or icing will ooze out when you squeeze. Close the bag by folding the side with the seam over to the plain side twice.

When ready to pipe, snip off the very end of the point. When not in use, wrap the piping bag in a plastic bag to prevent the icing from drying out.

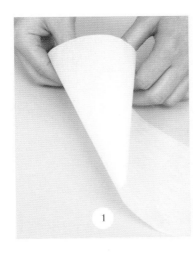
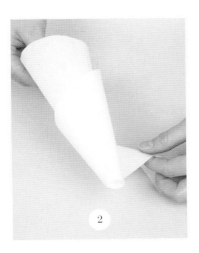

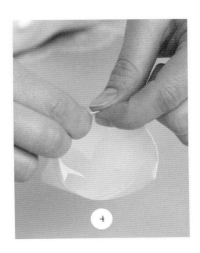

QUANTITY GUIDES

Cake-mix quantities Use the total weight of the ingredients of each basic recipe as a starting point to work out the amount of cake mixture required. The suggested weights below have been precisely calculated and are used in our kitchen. However, they may vary depending on the outcome of your cake mixture and your oven. I recommend that you allow for a little more cake mixture than you need and test what works best for you. Note that the cake tins stated below need to be multiplied by the number of cake layers required for your cake.

Cake tin size Based on 1 round or square cake tin, 4cm high	Victoria sponge mix Weights are approximate and depend on the volume of your cake mixture	Chocolate cake mix Weights are approximate and depend on the volume of your cake mixture	Mini cakes	Cupcakes
10cm	100g	130g	makes 2	
15cm	250g	330g	makes 4	
20cm or 23cm garland ring pan	480g	560g	makes 8	
25cm or 30 x 20cm baking tray or 23cm Bavaria bundt cake tin	760g	900g	makes 12	makes 20–24
30cm or 15cm spherical cake tin	1.25kg	1.5kg	makes 18	

Quantity guide for fruit cake mixture

20cm round: 2 x the basic recipe; baking time 3–4 hours
25cm round: 3 x the basic recipe; baking time 4–5 hours
30cm: 5 x the basic recipe; baking time 5–6 hours

Buttercream, ganache, marzipan and sugar paste quantities Use the quantities below as a guide to the approximate amounts required for a standard round or square tiered cake made with 3 layers, each about 10cm high.

Cake/base board size	Buttercream/ganache	Marzipan/sugar paste	Sugar paste for baseboard
10cm	250g	400g	
15cm	350g	600g	300g
20cm	700g	800g	450g
25cm	1kg	1.2kg	600g
30cm	1.5kg	1.75kg	700g
35cm			800g

SUGAR FLOWER GLOSSARY

Here are a few specialist terms that I will refer to in the designs throughout this book.

Balling This technique is used to stretch a petal all over and give the edges a wavy appearance. It involves applying an even pressure using a ball tool or the rounded end of a Celstick, and moving it in a circular motion over the flower paste. To create a wavy petal edge, move half of the ball tool or Celstick on the petal edge and half on the petal foam pad. You can achieve the same results on smaller flowers or petals using a bone tool.

Colouring flower paste Always use food paste colours to dye flower paste, as they won't alter the consistency too much. If you are using a colour for the first time and you don't know how much to use, test it on a small piece of paste first to avoid wastage. Add the colour with a cocktail stick, dabbing it in little dots all over the paste, then knead it through from the outside to the middle, as though you were kneading dough. Wear thin rubber gloves when using dark colours, as it can take days to remove the colour from your hands. This will also avoid contaminating any lighter colours you may be using at the same time. When kneading, try to push any air out of the paste when folding it. Don't stretch and pull it like chewing gum as you may incorporate small air bubbles. Once the colour is mixed through, the paste may feel a bit stiff and sticky; if so, add a dab of white vegetable fat and knead until the paste becomes smooth and pliable. Once mixed, rest the paste in a sealable plastic bag for at least 15 minutes. This will allow the paste to firm up and the colour to develop. You may find that the colour darkens after a few hours, so start by making it a touch lighter than required.

Dusting This is the process of applying petal dust to sugar flowers and leaves with an artist's paintbrush. I use a selection of thin pointed brushes for lines and finer areas, and wide flat brushes to dust wider sections on a petal. The brushing technique varies from flower to flower; however, as a general rule, you will achieve the most natural effects by brushing from the edge of the petal or leaf towards the middle. Before brushing, chop up the colour grains with your brush so that the dust is fine and powdery. Before applying it to the petal or leaf, make sure you don't have too much dust clinging onto your brush, as this can make the colour look patchy and messy. To clean your brushes, dab them in cornflour. It is helpful to have a sheet of tissue paper to hand to wipe excess colour off the brush. Fine colour specks of dust are almost invisible to the eye and can travel further than you think. I recommend cleaning your work area thoroughly after dusting, and make sure you don't have white iced cakes sitting near the dusting area.

Dusting colour/petal dust This is a powdered form of food colour which is used, as the name suggests, for dusting sugar flowers and leaves. There is a huge variety of petal dust colours available; however, not all powdered colours are edible, so make sure you check the packaging before use. Some of the colours I use are made for the use of sugar flowers but, due to the recent changes in UK food-colour legislation, they are no longer classed as food safe. These are non-toxic craft dusts; any flowers made using craft dust must be removed from a cake before eating. You can mix different petal dusts to create your own colours, or dilute them with white petal dust to make them paler.

Edible glue This is used to stick flower paste petals and leaves together. It has a clear thick gel-like consistency, and you can either buy it ready made, or make your own. I make mine by mixing a heaped teaspoon of gum tragacanth with about 180ml of water, but you can use CMC or tylose powder instead. At first, the powder will be lumpy; stir it occasionally to make the mixture swell up to a thick glue. I store mine in the fridge where, if kept in a clean container and used only with clean utensils, it can last for several weeks. You should dispose of the glue when tiny black spots of mould start to show. Another alternative is to pour a small amount of hot water from the kettle over a piece of flower paste and stir it until it dissolves. Once it starts to cool, it will thicken to a glue.

Flower picks These are little plastic tubes used for inserting wired sugar flowers into cakes. Wires can be a health and safety hazard and should never be pushed into a cake directly. When making a cake with wired sugar flowers for resale, always provide the customer with a delivery note stating that the sugar flowers come with non-edible wires that must be removed before eating. Flower picks can also be used for fresh flowers that are being used to decorate a cake.

Florist tape This is a waxy, stretchy paper ribbon that is wrapped around florist wires (see below) to give them a neat finish, and to tape flowers and leaves together. It is available in different shades of green and in white and its waxy texture makes it stick to a wire by itself if you pull it tight when you wrap it around a wire. You can buy it in widths of about 7mm or 15mm. I tend to buy 15mm tape and cut it in half lengthways before use. The easiest way to do this is to wrap the tape over 2 fingers, flatten it, then cut it into a thinner strip. You will find it much easier and neater to use this way.

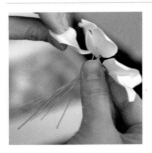

Florist wire Florist wires are used to make wired sugar flowers and leaves. They are available in a selection of green shades and white and come in different thicknesses, usually ranging from 18 gauge to about 30 gauge. The lower the number, the thicker the wire; as a rule of thumb, the larger and heavier the flower, the thicker the wire that is required. Most individually wired petals and leaves are made using 26- and 28-gauge wires; stems for large flowers, such as roses, are typically made with 20- or 22-gauge wires. As florist wires are not edible, they need to be removed from the cake before eating.

Frilling Using a bulbous cone modelling tool, or the pointed end of a Celstick, frilling is the term for creating a petal edge with lots of tiny ruched waves. To frill a petal, place it on a smooth non-stick plastic board lightly dusted with cornflour. Place the thick part of the frilling tool or Celstick on the petal edge with the tip pointing towards the middle, then move it back and forth, applying a little pressure, until the edges start to frill. Move the tool onto the next section and repeat until the entire edge looks frilly.

Mexican hat A Mexican hat is the term for a sombrero-shaped piece of paste at the back of a sugar flower. When I started learning to make sugar flowers, I was taught to make them by hand using a rolling pin. Luckily, these days you can buy non-stick plastic boards that have holes in for making different sizes of Mexican hat as you roll out the paste over the top. The purpose of a Mexican hat is to give the flower a strong centre to either attach a wire to or create a neck or trumpet shape, or both. The Mexican hat should always be as large as possible for maximum strength, so place your flower cutter on top of the holes on the board to check which one fits best.

Pencil vein This is a raised line that runs centrally across the back of a sugar flower petal or leaf. It is used for wiring individual petals or leaves. To make a petal or leaf with a pencil vein, you simply roll out the flower paste over the ridges of a veining board. When cutting out a petal or leaf, place the cutter over the vein with the thicker end at the bottom and the thinner end at the top.

Stamen Stamen used for sugar flower making are small wired bunches of pollen that come in a variety of sizes, shapes and colours. They are non-edible and must be removed before eating the cake. They are available at most cake-decorating shops and sugarcraft suppliers.

Steaming Steaming dusted sugar flowers and leaves will enhance their colour and add a subtle sheen to them, which makes them look even more realistic. It also makes the colour last longer. Use a kettle or a small saucepan of water on a light simmer to create the steam. Hold the flower over the steam (taking care not to burn your fingers) for about 3 seconds until it has a subtle sheen, then let it dry for a few minutes. Don't hold the flower too close to the water as little splashes can stain the petals.

Veining Using either a silicone veiner, a veining mat, a veining tool or a Dresden tool, veining is the term for embossing delicate lines into a flower paste petal or leaf to make it look more realistic. Place the flower, petal or leaf on a foam pad and run a veining tool or veining stick across the paste with some pressure. If using a veining mat, press it down on the entire surface of the petal or leaf to emboss the veined effect. Both methods may require the petal or leaf edge to be reshaped with a ball tool or bone tool afterwards, as the paste will become slightly flattened during the process.

White vegetable fat Mixed with flower paste to make it smooth and pliable, but also to lightly grease tools and equipment such as rolling pins, plastic boards and silicone veiners to prevent them from sticking to the paste.

SUPPLIERS

Most of the equipment and ingredients used to create the cakes and sugar flowers in this book are available from specialist cake decorating suppliers and, increasingly, the more everyday items can be found in supermarkets and general cookware shops.

My own website – www.peggyporschen.com – includes an online shop where you can purchase specialist cake decorating tools and ingredients, as well as an assortment of cookie cutters and other bakeware products. In addition, there is a small selection of handmade jams and exclusive loose-leaf tea blends available from our giftshop.

Throughout the year, I run a series of classes at the Peggy Porschen Academy. So whether you want to perfect your piping techniques to create irresistible cookies or brush up your baking skills to make heavenly cupcakes decorated with posies of spring flowers, there is a suitable course.

Peggy Porschen Academy

30 Elizabeth Street

Belgravia

London SW1W 9RB

www.peggyporschen.com

Each morning my team of specialist bakers freshly bake a range of layer cakes, cupcakes, cookies and other yummy delights for visitors to the Peggy Porschen Parlour to either enjoy there and then with an artisan tea blend or coffee to to take away for a teatime treat. If you have enjoyed the recipes in this book, I hope you will pay us a visit.

Peggy Porschen Parlour

116 Ebury Street

Belgravia

London SW1W 9QQ

www.peggyporschen.com

The publisher would like to thank Sanderson for the floral fabrics and wallpapers used throughout this book.
www.sanderson-uk.com

Publishing Director **Jane O'Shea**
Commissioning Editor **Lisa Pendreigh**
Project Editor **Katie Golsby**
Copy Editor **Kathy Steer**
Creative Director **Helen Lewis**
Art Direction and Design **Helen Bratby**
Photographer **Georgia Glynn Smith**
Stylist **Vicky Sullivan**
Production Director **Vincent Smith**
Production Controller **Leonie Kellman**

First published in 2014 by Quadrille Publishing Ltd
Alhambra House, 27–31 Charing Cross Road, London WC2H 0LS
www.quadrille.co.uk

Text, recipes, cake designs and illustrations
© 2014 Peggy Porschen
Photography © 2014 Georgia Glynn Smith
Artwork, design and layout © 2014 Quadrille Publishing Ltd

British Library Cataloguing-in-Publication Data
A catalogue record for this book is available
from the British Library

ISBN 978 184949 373 4

Printed in China

INDEX

ACKNOWLEDGEMENTS

Cakes in Bloom has been my absolute favourite – as well as most challenging – work to date. I couldn't be more thrilled with the result and it's all thanks to the joint team effort of the amazingly talented and dedicated people that I have had the pleasure of working with. Firstly, I would like to thank my publisher, Quadrille, for giving me the opportunity to lay my love and passion for sugar flowers down on paper. In particular I would like to thank Alison Cathie, Jane O'Shea, Lisa Pendreigh and Helen Lewis. It's been an amazing experience creating this book and I'd like to thank all of you for your help and support.

I am very lucky to have some true stars amongst my team at Peggy Porschen: My dearest Naomi, how could I have done this book without your support. Thank you for doing an amazing job, for keeping me on track at photo shoots, for recording every little cutter, colour and modelling tool used in the book, and for contributing some of the most remarkable flowers. Sweet Olivia, you also have been a great help and wonderful support to me and Naomi, thank you so much! Thank you Cinthia for coming to the rescue when extra help was needed, it was great we had one more chance to working together before you moved back home to Brazil.

A big thank you to the production team at Peggy Porschen Cakes, for keeping the ship afloat and business as usual while we all were busy with *Cakes in Bloom*. Stephanie, you have done an amazing job as always! Thank you for all your hard work, advice and inspiration. And for sharing my vision and enthusiasm for this book.

Here's to the the creatives of *Cakes in Bloom* who have helped to pull the whole thing together: Georgia Glynn Smith, thank you, thank you, thank you for the most fabulous photography. I know you pushed yourself as hard as I did and the images speak for themselves. Vicky Sullivan, your styling was absolutely beautiful. And all this while being very pregnant! Thank you ever so much. Helen Bratby, thank you for designing such a beautiful book. I love all the special touches and it's been a real pleasure working with you.

Last but not least, I owe a big hug and kiss to my two boys. My husband Bryn and our son Max. Thank you Bryn for looking after Max while I was away shooting, and for bringing him on set to delight us all with his cute smiles. I couldn't have imagined a nicer distraction, and nor could the girls.